EVERY STEP
YOU TAKE

EVERY STEP YOU TAKE

A Memoir

Jock Soto

with Leslie Marshall

HARPER

An Imprint of HarperCollins*Publishers*
www.harpercollins.com

The names and identifying characteristics of some individuals discussed in this book have been changed to protect their privacy.

HarperCollins books may be purchased for educational, business, or sales promotional use. For information, please write: Special Markets Department, HarperCollins Publishers, 10 East 53rd Street, New York, NY 10022.

FIRST EDITION

Designed by Renato Stanisic

Library of Congress Cataloging-in-Publication Data
Soto, Jock.
  Every step you take : a memoir / Jock Soto.—1st ed.
    p. cm.
  ISBN 978-0-06-173238-6 (hardback) 1. Soto, Jock. 2. Ballet dancers—United States—Biography. I. Title.
  GV1785.S645A3 2011
  792.8028092—dc22
  [B]

                              2011012725

11 12 13 14 15   OV/RRD   10 9 8 7 6 5 4 3 2 1

For Mama Jo and Papa Joe,
for my family all across this beautiful country,
to the love of my life, Luis Fuentes,
and to our two ever-faithful dogs, Tristan and Bandit,
woof and arf back at ya.

Contents

EVERY STEP
YOU TAKE

CHAPTER ONE

Prelude

*The past is part of the present, just as the
future is. We exist in time.*
— GEORGE BALANCHINE

I will never forget that hot summer day in 2004 when Peter
Martins, ballet master in chief for the New York City
Ballet, asked me if I would come talk with him about something important. We were in the Saratoga Performing Arts
Center, where the NYCB has a visiting performance schedule every summer, and I had just danced a matinee performance of Balanchine's ballet *Stravinsky Violin Concerto*. I
was sweaty and tired and had only a few hours before I had to
get ready for an evening performance of Balanchine's *Agon*,
but I dragged myself upstairs to find Peter in the stuffy little
room he uses as his temporary office when the company is in
Saratoga Springs.

When I entered the room, Peter—a tall, blond, and very
noble Dane—jumped up to greet me with a great big bear
hug, as he always does when we meet. For close to a quarter

of a century I had been having meetings of this kind with Peter to discuss upcoming performances, and in recent years our respective roles in these meetings had evolved. For the first two decades of my career, Peter had done almost all the talking, strategizing about how I could expand my repertoire and what ballets I might dance, while I listened quietly. But in the last five years I had found myself doing more and more of the talking when we met, updating Peter on the current status of my injuries and ailments and strategizing about what I therefore could *not* dance. I didn't know exactly what Peter wanted to talk about on that particular day, but as I stepped back to take a seat on a sofa in the corner, I could see that Peter was unusually excited about something. As soon as I was seated he delivered his news.

"I have decided on the program for your farewell performance," Peter announced. "You will dance Balanchine, Robbins, Wheeldon, Martins, and Taylor-Corbett. Five ballets. It will be a first in the history of the NYCB!" he added, waving a finger in the air. "Nobody has ever done this." My eyes just sort of bulged, and I gave an uneasy giggle. Five ballets? That evening I called my mother in Santa Fe and said, "Mom, I believe Peter wants to kill me when I retire."

The physical challenges of the program Peter described to me on that summer day in Saratoga were definitely daunting. But what probably hit me harder was the emotional shock of hearing him pronounce the actual ballets and confirm the exact date—June 19, 2005—for the program that would be my very last performance as a principal dancer with the New York City Ballet. The decision to retire had been mine, and I was confident that the time was right. But dancing was all

I had ever done in life. I had started at age three when I performed ceremonial dances with my Native American mother on the Navajo Reservation in Arizona, where my family lived. At age five I began my formal ballet training in Phoenix; at age thirteen I moved to New York to attend the School of American Ballet, the famous ballet institution founded in 1934 by the philanthropist Lincoln Kirstein and the legendary dancer and choreographer George Balanchine; when I was sixteen Balanchine invited me to join the New York City Ballet, and I had been dancing there ever since. I was closing in on forty, and the only thing I had ever done—literally for as much as eleven or twelve hours a day, six days a week, for my entire life—was about to end. Just like that, after one last performance, on June 19, 2005.

At some point every professional dancer has to make the difficult decision to stop performing, and for me this decision had come after nearly a decade of the escalating injuries and joint pain that inevitably come with advancing age. A few months before my meeting with Peter in Saratoga Springs, I had plunked myself down on the red leather sofa in Peter's office at Lincoln Center and announced my decision to retire. I wanted to step offstage voluntarily while I was still strong, with a positive plan for the next phase of my life. I didn't want someone to have to tell me it was time to go—or, even worse, read about it in the newspaper, or overhear someone whispering about it in the hallways. I had picked the age of forty as my deadline, and I was going to stick to it. I knew it was time. But as Peter rattled off those names on that hot summer day—Balanchine, Robbins, Wheeldon, Martins, and Taylor-Corbett—everything suddenly seemed so real

and so final. Five beautiful ballets—and then nothing. The
process seemed as sudden and irreversible as a violent death.

The good news was that I had almost a full year to get used
to the idea of retirement and to condition and strengthen my
body for the marathon dance feat Peter had described. The
bad news was that this gave me a nice long time to be anxious
and worried about everything. What if an injury knocked me
out and there was no farewell performance? What if I collapsed halfway through? What if nobody came?

Something else had begun weighing heavily on me that
same year. In 2003 my mother had been diagnosed with colon
cancer, and her treatment was not going well. She had had
two operations already, and new tumors kept being discovered. The realization that she might not necessarily live forever had shocked me, and for the first time I was thinking
back over the choices I had made thus far in my life, wondering if I might have made some mistakes.

I started life on the same reservation in Arizona where my
mother—a full-blooded Native American—had been born
and raised, and I spent the first twelve years of my life in the
Southwest with my parents and my older brother, Kiko. But
by the age of fourteen I was living on my own in New York
City, pursuing my dream to become a great dancer. I had a
full scholarship as a student at the School of American Ballet
(SAB)—and nothing else. Housing, food, education—the
basic foundations of a normal teenager's life—had not been
put in place for me, but I didn't care. I was happy to improvise
on these fronts. All I wanted in life was to dance.

I never did live with my parents and older brother again.
In fact, for almost three decades I rarely saw them. After

learning about my mother's illness in 2003, haunted by the thought of the many years I had missed being with my family, I began spending any vacation time I had with my parents. At the time, they were living outside Santa Fe, in a trailer situated on the grounds of the fenced-in A-1 Self Storage facility that they were managing. Whenever I was visiting we would close the gates at 5:00 p.m., locking ourselves inside the storage facility for the night, and then our evening ritual would begin. My father, who is a full-blooded, *muy* macho Puerto Rican, would watch his television (at very high volume, almost always tuned to either a war movie or a news segment about war); I would make myself an evening cocktail and begin to cook our dinner; and my beautiful Navajo princess of a mother would regale me with stories about my Native American heritage.

"The most important thing in life is family," Mom kept saying to me, over and over during the course of my visits. I would nod, and do my best to listen and absorb what she was saying as I continued to cook. At a certain point—and in large part to reassure my mother that I was doing my best to preserve these stories about our heritage—I began working with a filmmaker named Gwendolen Cates on a documentary that would trace our family background and my career in dance.

Making the documentary proved to be engaging in ways I hadn't expected—for the first time I was pausing to look backward at my childhood and my family history. But the project also added to my anxieties during the final days with the NYCB in ways I hadn't anticipated. For starters, making a film is time-consuming, complicated, and expensive. And then there was this other troubling obstacle the process of making the film had unearthed: a huge wall of resistance inside me. The truth was, I wasn't sure I really wanted to examine my Navajo *or* my Puerto Rican "roots." I had worked so hard to leave those worlds behind, and I didn't want to go back. I wanted to move forward into a future for which I was already making very specific plans. In 2003 I had met a dashing sommelier and chef, Luis Fuentes, and I was excited about our life together. I have always loved to cook, and Luis and I had dreams of starting a catering business or a restaurant someday. I was determined to hit the ground running when I retired, and at Luis's suggestion I enrolled at the Institute of Culinary Education for classes that started the day after my final performance. I wasn't going to miss a beat. I was going to orchestrate every detail of my retirement methodically, as I might rehearse the intricate movements of the most complex ballet, reviewing every step, over and over, until the process of transition from principal dancer to ex-dancer had been loaded right into my flesh and bones—a fluid series of movements internalized by my body, no longer thought about but simply performed. One day dancer, next day not. No big deal. Pass the salt.

Despite all my calm and deliberate planning, when the last week before my final performance finally arrived I was a wreck—anxious and confused, and overwhelmed by a variety of feelings. Several of my family members had traveled east early for the event, and while their presence strengthened the sense of support I felt, it also compounded my anxiety about performing well. For several of them the long trip to New York was the first travel of this kind they had ever made, and I wanted to make sure they felt it had been worthwhile. A longtime ballet patron and friend, Anne Bass, incredibly generous as always, had offered to host a party in my honor after the performance, so she and I were busy coordinating details for a Mexican feast for 450 to be held downtown in a party space called Industria. I was working night and day with the physical therapists and my trainer to hold my exhausted and vulnerable body together, and at the same time rehearsing not just for my farewell performance but also for the regular ballet program pieces I was dancing in the days leading up to my performance. Everything felt pretty crazy.

When June 19 finally arrived I was numb. Luis very kindly took me out for brunch before the performance, which was scheduled as a 3:00 p.m. matinee, but I couldn't even touch my food. As the hour approached, I sat in my dressing room and stared in the mirror, looking for evidence of something new in my face that might reflect the extreme change my life was about to take. I applied my stage makeup for the last time—a little eyeliner and a little blush—and dressed and headed down to the stage earlier than usual. Standing in the wings, looking out into the theater, I realized it seemed surreal to me that today would be the last time that I would throw my whole heart and soul out across this familiar platform, where I had danced so many amazing stories. A wave of panic swept through me as I considered the possibility that I wouldn't make it through the program—I had rehearsed the steps of all five ballets over and over, but never back-to-back while dancing full out in the real-time performance framework. (Dancers my age rarely rehearse a ballet dancing full out—if you do, you would have nothing left by performance time.) What if my legs just gave out halfway through? The possibility was horrifying.

Finally the moment came for the program to begin. As I stood in the wings, I found it strange to think that at the end of this evening the person I had been for thirty-five years—the obsessed and driven ballet dancer—would just disappear. Where would that person go? And what would be left in the space he had once occupied? I looked out to find my family in the third-row orchestra seats below, and caught my mother's eye. She was beautiful in the red shirt and black pants and jacket she had made for herself for the occasion, and she was wearing one of the wigs—the short, spiky one that was my favorite—she had started using since chemotherapy. As our eyes met she sent me the huge smile that had warmed and brightened my life for as long as I could remember, and I felt a familiar calmness spreading though me. It was time to dance.

I made the sign of the cross—something I had done before every ballet I ever performed—and took a deep breath. As the music began I stepped onto the stage and into the role of Bernardo of the Sharks in the "Dance at the Gym" scene from Jerome Robbins's *West Side Story Suite*. I turned to my fellow Sharks as we advanced upon Riff and his gang of Jets. "Mambo, mambo, mambo!" I shouted. In a matter of seconds, the combination of music and movement gathered me up and carried me to a new place. Any concerns I had had about a dancer named Jock Soto and the possible pitfalls of his retirement performance evaporated. I was a Shark, and I was at war.

TO MY GREAT relief my entire retirement program unfolded as it was meant to, and in the months that followed

I congratulated myself for having executed the whole transition successfully, more or less as I had planned it. I was really enjoying teaching full-time at the SAB and taking courses at the Institute for Culinary Education. The last pieces of the documentary about me, titled *Water Flowing Together*, seemed to be finally falling into place, and Luis and I loved getting to spend more time with each other and with Tristan, the adorable baby basset hound my fellow dancers had given me as a retirement present. In fact, other people seemed to be more traumatized by my retirement than I was.

"Don't you miss performing?" they would ask me incredulously when I bumped into them on the street. "Yes, I do miss performing. It's all the other hours I don't miss," I would say, trying to brush it off lightly. "I'm tired. I'm so ready to do something else." And I believed this to be true.

But deep inside, I know part of me must have been in shock. There is no greater feeling than the one that comes after a performance when everything has gone incredibly well. In the last decade of my career, when I was dancing so much with Wendy Whelan, I often felt that our dancing must be the closest thing there was to flying. Our beings and our bodies merged, and we went soaring through the ballet on a cloud. Every time we danced together it felt like a new story was unfolding. Of course I missed it, and knowing I was letting go of this experience forever had been like watching a part of myself die. In so many ways, on so many levels it seemed unthinkable—so I did my best not to think about it.

At the same time that I was keeping myself in studied denial about the death of my professional identity, I was trying to face a much more serious and upsetting loss. My mother's health had continued to disintegrate, and she was getting weaker and weaker. Even though she was often living as much as three thousand miles away, I had always remained aware of my mother as a powerful and vital force in my life and in the world. It was not just her physical presence—her beautiful skin and hair, elegant face and carriage—or her warm and embracing manner that struck everyone who met her. Mom had certain ways about her—ways of seeing and ways of speaking and ways of teaching and loving and living—that were unique. Born and raised on her clan's ancestral lands on the Navajo tribal reservation near Chinle, Arizona, she was both humble and proud, and filled with an innate courage and dignity. She had often talked about how her elders on the reservation had taught her to "walk in beauty and in harmony," and I knew she had a grand scheme for how life—whether on or off the reservation—should be led by all of us. And now this amazingly intense and vibrant woman was fading, beaten down by rounds and rounds of chemotherapy and all its nasty side effects.

I was grateful that my retirement allowed me to spend more time with Mom, but I found that the more I saw her the more I dreaded losing her. Over the months, another potential loss began to haunt me. My mother had always been the bookkeeper and historian in our family. I was afraid that if she died there would be much—about my parents and grandparents and their families, about my own early childhood, about my mother's Navajo heritage and my father's life in Puerto Rico—that would go to the grave with her. I had promised Mom that I would try to remember what she had told me about our heritage, and do my best to pass it along. But what if I wanted to learn more about my past at some point? Who would I turn to?

Recognizing how much I didn't know about my parents' backgrounds and my own early years brought me face-to-face with an even more alarming question: Did I even know my own life, the one I had supposedly lived for the past thirty years here in New York? Luis and I had begun to talk about getting married someday, and maybe even having a family. If I ever had children of my own, would I be able to tell them about this life I had lived, what I had done and what I had learned from it? Or had I danced right over three decades of precious time, pouring everything into the stories I was creating onstage and ignoring the overall arc of how everything, onstage and offstage, fits together? This raised another troubling question, especially for someone facing the challenge of inventing a whole new life: Can you figure out where you are going if you have never paused to consider where you came from or where you have been?

I had been so determined to channel all my energies forward into a productive future after retiring—yet now I found myself possessed by a curiosity about my past. I kept thinking about the months and months that had piled up into years and years, during which my only focus had been a near maniacal pursuit of the art of dance. Balanchine's famous quote about ballet came to mind: "The past is part of the present, just as the future is. We exist in time." Could I apply his comment on dance to life in general? Could I keep moving through the present and planning for the future, and at the same time be able to rewind the tape and sift through my past, looking for any information and insights that might be embedded in all those days and weeks and months and years during which I had just floated through life—happily adrift in a universe that was all about dancing, dancing, dancing?

For a long time I wrestled with these questions, wondering if I had the courage and stamina and honesty—not to mention intellectual depth—to actually harvest anything from a more probing look at my life. But on the sad day in March 2008 when my brave mother finally lost her battle with cancer and died, something shifted inside me. I didn't recognize the change instantly, but over the next few weeks it became obvious that I had been asking myself certain questions for long enough. The time had come to try to find some answers.

CHAPTER TWO

The Sleeping Beauty

Every day the world turns upside down for
someone who is sitting on top of it.
—ELLEN GILCHRIST, *IN THE LAND OF DREAMY DREAMS*

I am three years old, and I am dancing with my mother. I am three, and she is immortal—as big and beautiful and bright as the sun in the sky. We are dressed in special dancing clothes that she has made for us. I have little beaded moccasins and a headband of wiry horsehair; my velvet loincloth and matching fringed vest with sparkling sequins are a pretty purple. We are carrying smooth circles that never start and never end, beautiful wooden hoops (mine are small and just my size, and my mother's are bigger, just right for her) made by my grandfather.

As we begin to move through our dance steps, holding our hoops, my mother and I become another set of hoops. We roll, separate but connected, inside the heat and the light and inside the irresistible beat of my grandfather's drum and the sound of his voice as he chants a long, special song. We gather momentum and unity as we move; the surrounding light and colors and all of the familiar smells—horsehair, leather, dust, hot clay—become one with our movement and the drumbeat and my grandfather's voice. I notice from the corner of my eye that even the sunlight is dancing with us now, its shadow feet rushing to match the movement of every step we take, meeting us toe-to-toe with perfect timing.

I am dancing with my mother and I am only three, but already I can feel the thrill and the power of surrendering to the sum of our partnership with each other and with everything in this moment in time. I am her son, she is my sun, I am a small moon in her happy orbit. Every time we dance it is like this—we spin ourselves a brand-new universe.

Whenever I dive into the murk of my childhood years, the earliest artifact I can bring back to the surface is this memory of my mother teaching me the traditional Navajo hoop dance. As memories go, my childhood pas de deux with Mom is always easy to find—in fact, over the years it has revisited me often, bringing with it sensations so vivid and visceral they register more like a current than a recollected experience. On March 28, 2008, as I sit in an uncomfortable wooden pew in a small chapel in Colorado Springs and try to listen to the rent-a-priest who is speaking at my mother's memorial service, the memory comes to me once more—this time in an act of emotional rescue.

My beautiful mother—Josephine Towne Soto—has died. But as the gray minutes roll past and the priest at the front of the chapel drones on, my beautiful mother is still dancing with me in a world of bright light and vivid colors. We are moving across the hard-packed earth in front of my grandpa

Bud and grandma Rachel's hogan on the Navajo Reservation in Chinle, Arizona, on a day four decades ago, but we are also dancing through the fluid dimension of time, on a platform that is both of and above the world we usually inhabit. This is what the two of us always have done together; this is what we always will do. My mother was my very first dance partner, and as I close my eyes and ears to the grim little gathering that surrounds me, it is a great relief to know that I will be dancing with her forever.

Only two weeks have passed since the moment when my brother, Kiko, called me, as I was headed to teach my partnering class at the School of American Ballet in New York, to say I'd better come back to Colorado Springs, where Mom had been admitted to hospice care several weeks earlier. We have been through many tough times since our mother was diagnosed with cancer five years ago—but nothing could have prepared me for these final weeks, when every twenty-four hours seemed to bring brutal new diminishments of her autonomy. For me the visual and emotional horrors of watching my mother suffer a slow and painful death have been compounded by the strange and unpredictable dynamics of our large and unruly family. My mother has always been the powerful and beloved center of that family, both the immediate and the extended branches. Not one of us wanted to let her go. As we all have tried to face the pain of our profound loss, spoken and unspoken feelings have ricocheted like stray bullets among the scattered members of this communication-challenged family. My father has been retreating deeper and deeper into a childlike state of denial that I find frustrating, but even worse are the tensions that have developed between my immediate family members who left the reservation some years ago, and my mother's traditional Navajo relatives who still live there. The telephone calls between us have grown more and more strained.

Living in my own world far away in New York City for so many years, I sometimes forget the imposing scale of our "clan." But whenever I am back home, it hits me—we are a big family. My mother was the second eldest of nine children born to my Navajo grandparents, Rachel Begay Towne and Joseph Towne, and the second of seven daughters—Alice; my mother, Josephine; Buddieta; Rosita; Valerie; Pauline; and Yvonne. Next came the long-awaited boy, Orlando, and finally another girl, Rochelle. Over the years, my mother— always the rebel, always the traveler—established herself as the most colorful and also the most controversial among this brood. For starters, the majority of her siblings have remained on or near the reservation, where they were all born, in keeping with Navajo tradition. But at a young age Mom began to roam to faraway places, and over the years she established a pattern of moving on and off the reservation that upset her more traditional relatives. When she was only eighteen Mom fell in love with my father, a full-blooded Puerto Rican named José Soto, and not much later she made a big break with Navajo tradition by marrying outside the tribe—a huge taboo and another source of ongoing friction with her relatives. Now, to complicate matters, my mother requested that she be cremated and buried on land Luis and I had recently bought in Eagle Nest, New Mexico—thereby resoundingly rejecting the Navajo tradition of burial in which the intact body is returned to its

Native soil in a three-day-long, highly ritualized ceremony that involves the entire clan.

Mom was a beloved member of a big clan, but as I look around the little chapel we have chosen for her memorial service I note that the pews are nearly empty. My brother, Kiko, and his wife, Deb, are on one side of me, and my partner, Luis, and my father are on the other. Luis is holding my hand, squeezing it, as I look around at a few friends of Kiko's and my father's who dot the pews. Not one of Mom's siblings has come to this service. Throughout the previous week, as it became clearer and clearer that her death was imminent, I had been calling all of them to tell them that it was time to come see her and say their good-byes. In our phone conversations my Navajo relatives made it clear that all of Mom's untraditional decisions about her burial were causing considerable upset back on the reservation where her family members and elders had been planning a traditional Navajo burial and ceremony. In the end only three of Mom's eight siblings—her sisters Rosie, Buddy, and Ali—managed the trip to Colorado Springs to say good-bye to her. When they were in Kiko's house it had seemed to me that these sisters scuttled about with dark, disapproving looks, and when they visited my mother in her hospice room they stood in a circle and held hands and chanted and prayed. After being there for two days, they took off furtively in the middle of the night, saying only a brief good-bye.

I had been upset by all of this, and I became even more upset when I heard from family members that the elders on the reservation had started planning a memorial service for Mom before she had even died. I stomped around and cursed my Navajo relatives. You would think a family could pull together in times of such sadness and trauma. All of this was hard enough; did they have to make it harder? Outwardly I criticized my relatives for their selfish behavior, but on some level I was also nervous about the situation. As a resident of New York City for thirty years I have become well versed in metropolitan culture and all the sophistications of modern life. But the power of Navajo beliefs and superstitions and the consequences of going against them have been impressed upon me all my life. For years I have carried a private (and for the most part unacknowledged) guilt at having left the reservation where my clan lived. As I sit at my mother's memorial service in a chapel that is far away from our clan's sacred homelands, I have to acknowledge that somewhere deep inside I know that the ancient Navajo laws are nothing to mess with. Thinking about this, I instinctively make the sign of the cross, the way I always used to before stepping onstage.

Looking around at the empty pews sends a painful reminder of another family situation that contributed to the pressure cooker atmosphere in Kiko's house during the last two weeks of my mother's life. Because of recent disagreements between Kiko and his ex-wife, their two sons, Trevor and Bryce (my mother's only grandchildren), have not been speaking to Kiko—or to any of us. Trevor and Bryce have not come to their grandmother's funeral. I called earlier in the week and left a voice message at their house, asking if my mother could please see her grandsons before she died. Kiko's ex-wife left a short and bitter response on Kiko's voice mail: "Everyone dies."

Everyone dies, yes. But not everyone dies with the dignity and courage and grace of my Navajo princess of a mother. Several times in the past few days I have found myself back in the moment when I entered my mother's room at Pikes Peak Hospice for the last time. The curtains are drawn. The room looks impeccable—cleaner than when I left it to go grab a little lunch a while ago. The oxygen tank that has been her constant companion is no longer there. Mom is lying with her arms crossed underneath her favorite faux-fur blanket, which I bought her one Christmas from Pottery Barn. She looks beautiful, still and peaceful as a Sleeping Beauty. The strained and erratic breathing that I watched for five hours that same morning—counting the seconds between each gasp as I talked to her, touched her cheeks, held her hand—has stopped.

She looks so lovely and peaceful lying there, that on an impulse I kneel down beside her bed and gently kiss her, allowing myself the wild hope that maybe, just maybe, she will magically awaken and give me her amazing smile. But she does not.

It is 4:30 on the afternoon of March 25, 2008, and Josephine Towne Soto, my beloved mother, has departed. There is nothing bendable or flexible or fixable about this sad fact. Nothing to do but say good-bye and leave. Looking around the room, I spot my mother's favorite red bathrobe on a chair. I gather the bathrobe in a tight ball against my chest to take back to New York with me, and then I pick up her laptop computer, which has been waiting like a faithful pet at the foot of her bed. As I cast one last look at my mother's peaceful silhouette, it occurs to me that my mother has managed her own death with the same aplomb with which she managed everything in our family all my life. I understand that she didn't want us to have to watch her lose the breath of life and depart. She has chosen to slip away quietly and quickly, while she was alone.

At the memorial the priest is still talking, and my eyes wander to a poster-size picture of Mom—an enlarged version of a photograph that my father has carried in his wallet for more than two decades—on display in the chapel. In the picture Mom has short hair, much like one of the wigs she wore in the last few years because of chemotherapy. This gets me thinking about Mom's hair—she had the most beautiful long dark hair, thick and lustrous. I remember how when I was younger she would pile it up into a beehive. A moment later I am a child again, riding in my father's '65 convertible Cadillac. In the front seat Mom is snuggling up close to my father as he drives. Kiko and I are in the backseat, eating candy and carefully stashing the wrappers in Mom's beehive. We giggle. We know she won't find them until sometime after she gets to work.

Thinking about how much I used to love to touch my mother's beautiful hair when I was young, I am suddenly reliving another day, when I am ten and I have asked Mom if she would feather my hair. When she finishes, I am thrilled. I think I look incredible. A male Farrah Fawcett. I put on my roller skates and go outside, feeling like some sort of beauty queen. Me, my feathered hair, my skates. I glide through the streets of our little desert community. Just like a scene from the movie *Xanadu*. Clearly I am a homosexual already . . .

Everyone is standing up. Mom's service is finally over now, and as we are leaving the funeral facilities I notice a lone figure sitting at the back of a bigger, separate chapel that is near ours. The person looks familiar to me, and a moment later I realize it is Kiko's older son, Bryce. As soon as he sees that he has been spotted, Bryce takes off in a dead run. A second later Kiko takes off after him, calling his name and begging him to stop, to come back. As I watch them disappear down the road I wonder if everyone's family is as complicated as mine. Our mother has died. Can't we all just get along, for her sake?

My mother and father always shared a chronic restlessness—there were periods of their lives together when they moved to a new place every two or three months—and the day after Mom's memorial my father demonstrates that he may have lost a wife but he has not lost his urge to ramble. His RV has been parked in Kiko's driveway during these last weeks while Mom's been in the hospital, but now he is anxious to take off. He wants to get behind the wheel and hit the road, go somewhere. Luis and I decide to accompany Pop in the motor home on the three-hour trek to go see the house we are building in Eagle Nest, New Mexico. It is the house that I have promised to build for my mother since the age of six. It is the house we were finally building together. Except now it has become the house my mother will never see. It has become the house being built on the ground in which my mother wants her ashes to be buried.

While Pop is driving, Luis and I take a nice long nap, bouncing around on Mom and Pop's bed in the back bedroom of the RV. We lie there under the blankets, staring out at the Colorado Mountains, and then at the winding Rio Grande and into the New Mexican landscape beyond. I am lying on my mother's side of the bed. I bury my head into her pillow to see if I can smell her.

When we get to Eagle Nest we walk through the house with the builder, Eldon, and discuss everything that has been done and everything that must still be done. We talk toilets, countertops, flooring, doorknobs. It is hard to concentrate, or even to care. At one point as we are standing outside, Eldon looks up and points to a huge herd of elk gathered on the mountainside above us. I wish my mother could be here to see how beautiful they are—so big and strong. As I look at the elk it strikes me that the communal beauty and strength of the herd resemble that of Mom's big family—our clan. I can see my mother's face in the faces of her mother and father and in each of her siblings and even in the faces of her siblings' children—my grandparents and the sprawling army of aunts and uncles and cousins who, in the Navajo culture, are also called my mothers and fathers and brothers and sisters. I see my mother's face in all of these relatives, many of whom I barely know, and I see her face every time I look in a mirror. The strength and rich color of the elk, the way the members of the herd resemble one another and stay together and graze together, remind me of what Mom always said about our family—that we were bound to one another by forces beyond ourselves, and that we would be together always. I am beginning to understand her now, and I believe her. We are many and we are far-flung, but we will always be a family.

When I leave the house site I head back to my father's motor home and get ready to do some hard-core cooking in the tiny RV kitchen. This is what I always do when my family and I are together. It is what I always did with my surrogate family members when I was a teenager pursuing a dream in New York. It is what Luis and I do now, when we want to relax together. We cook. As I start to bustle around the little cooking space I remember how much I love cooking in the RV. It feels so contained and no-nonsense, so self-sufficient and cozy. I roll up my sleeves and get to work. I am going to start with some Tequila Courage Margaritas and some Killer Guacamole. And then I am going to make my mom's famous pork chops smothered in onions and tomatoes with yellow rice and black beans. This is a recipe my father's mother taught Mom. I know it will make us all feel better. We will still stay here in the RV beside the half-built house for Mama Jo and we will eat together.

For Mom's sake, and for our own, we will prove that we can still be a family.

Courage and Comfort on the Go

IN MY EARLY years with my family I spent much of my time not just moving from home to home but actually living in a home that moved. Recreational vehicles (RVs), campers, motor homes, trailers—we roamed all through the Southwest, and at the end of each day, to cap our wandering with something that made us feel cozy and homey, we would prepare and eat a wonderful meal.

I think one of the reasons RV meals are always so fun to prepare and taste so good is because they demand a special resourcefulness on the part of the cook. Limited space, limited burners, a makeshift supply of utensils and pots and pans—the inventive chef welcomes all of the challenges that come with on-the-road cooking. One of my favorite meals whenever we traveled was a recipe for pork chops my mother had learned from my father's mother. I still find it such a comforting meal, so simple and inexpensive—and I have discovered it is just as satisfying when cooked in a stationary home.

In my version of Mom's pork chops, I have added poblano peppers, because I love them, and a dash of cumin or curry. The pork chops are also good without these extras. Sometimes if Luis is working late and I want to take the edge off my solitude, I put on my pajamas, make myself a big ol' margarita, and cook two of these chops. I serve myself in a large bowl, wrap up in a blanket, and—with the dogs at my feet sniffing the goodness—dive in. Try it and don't feel guilty. We all deserve it!

Mama Jo's Pork Chops with Onions, Tomatoes, and Poblano Peppers

SERVES 4

2 large Spanish onions, diced

3 poblano peppers, seeded and diced

5 cloves garlic, chopped

8 boneless pork chops (about 1½ inches thick)

Goya Adobo seasoning

About 5 tablespoons olive oil

Salt

1 16-ounce can chopped tomatoes

1 cup chicken stock

1 package of Sazón (available in the international-food section of most grocery stores)

Pepper

Dash of cumin or curry powder (optional)

Peel and dice the onions, and seed and dice the poblanos. Set the onions and peppers aside. Chop the garlic and set aside.

Place the pork chops in a large bowl. Season them generously with Goya Adobo and about 3 tablespoons of olive oil. Set the seasoned chops aside.

Heat about 2 tablespoons of olive oil in a large heavy skillet on high heat. When it is nice and hot, sear the chops on both sides (about 3 to 5 minutes per side depending on the thickness, and in batches if necessary). Do not overcook or the chops will be like bricks! Set the seared chops aside on a plate to rest, leaving the heat on under the pan. Drain any excess oil from the pan, leaving about a tablespoon.

Add your diced onions and poblano peppers to the pan and sauté for about 5 minutes, salting them a little so they sweat. If you need more liquid, pour in a little chicken stock. Add the chopped garlic and sauté for about a minute. Pour in your canned tomatoes and chicken stock. Bring the sauce to a boil, and then reduce the heat to medium.

Now you can add the Sazón, salt and pepper to your taste, and cumin or curry if you like. Cover and let everything simmer for about 20 minutes, so all the flavors marry. Put your chops back in and cook for about 5 minutes, covered. Then turn the chops over and cook for about 5 more minutes. I can't stand my chops hard—there is nothing worse than a chop so tough you need a chain saw to cut it—so I sometimes take one out and slice the center. If the juices run a little pink I know I can turn the stove off and let everything sit, covered, for a few minutes.

This recipe will feed four generously—or six to eight if you have light feeders—and can be served with yellow rice and beans or with plain white rice.

CHAPTER THREE

Fearful Symmetries

When you meet the mother, you understand the man.
—LOURDES LOPEZ, FORMER NYCB PRINCIPAL DANCER

When I came back to New York after my mother's memorial I brought only two of her possessions with me: her red bathrobe and her computer. I hung the bathrobe in a closet, pulling it out only occasionally for a quick sad sniff, and I stashed the computer way back in the darkest corner of the closet. During the last weeks of her life, Mom kept asking for her computer, even though she could no longer use her hands to type. I knew that in the past couple years she had been writing something that was important to her, stories about herself and about our family history. I knew she would want me to read whatever she had written. But I did not feel ready for this yet, and the sight of her abandoned computer made me sad.

During those first weeks back in New York I felt the way I am sure many people feel after the death of a parent: empty and numb. I was determined to move forward, and I was grateful to be able to throw myself into my teaching duties at the School of American Ballet and my cooking duties as a part-time caterer and my life with Luis and our two dogs, Tristan and Bandit. But as the days passed, a series of strange, almost hallucinatory flashes from my past began to ambush me in the most unlikely places. The subway, for instance, seemed to be a particularly fertile zone where almost anything could happen.

"Never whistle in the dark," the pneumatic doors whispered to me as they opened at a station stop. *"It will bring the bears,"* they added as they closed. Then a vision of my mother would come to me, smiling and laughing, sitting somewhere at dusk, surrounded by tall pine trees, the index finger of one hand across her lips and her other hand reaching out to cover mine. *"Never whistle in the dark, Jock. . . . It will bring the bears."*

Never whistle in the dark. And never point at the sun or at a rainbow—it is disrespectful. Be gentle with your food—the animals and plants have sacrificed themselves to feed you. Never walk in front of your elders. Listen, watch, and learn by example. Keep quiet. Enter the traditional eight-sided Navajo hogan through the east-facing door, and always move counterclockwise, around the hearth, to exit. All sorts of cryptic phrases and forgotten lessons, random shards from a life I had once lived, began to volunteer themselves at the oddest times. A tense memory I hadn't thought of in years—a moment when Kiko and I were hurried out of my grandparents' smoke-filled hogan by our mother when a visiting cousin fell to the ground with a river of strange words flowing from her mouth—returned to me with such ferocity as I was riding my bicycle home from Lincoln Center one evening that I had to dismount and lean, shaking, against a tree.

Old, forgotten smells returned to me, too. The yeasty smell of the seemingly infinite number of loaves of bread my grandmother Rachel baked in the clay oven outside my grandparents' shack, and the pungent, almost comforting smell of Grandma Rachel's whiskey breath as she said something to me in passing. The mouthwatering aroma of Navajo Fry Bread, a delicious, if not nutritious, treat that Kiko and I used to cook and sell at rodeos and powwows, operating our own little concession booth right alongside my parents' kachina doll and pottery booth. On certain days, when the wind and atmosphere were right, I thought I detected in the concrete canyons of New York the moist green promise of distant rain that used to come wafting to me over the hot desert from some lucky wet canyon miles and miles away.

These memories and sensations had not visited me for years. Was my mother sending them to me to remind me of the world I left behind when I had moved to New York? Was this her way of prodding me to make good on my promise to understand and honor our family history? Just in case, I decided I should write down everything I could remember from my mother's informal "heritage" sessions late in her life—but as it turned out, I had not retained much. I knew that the Navajo tribe called themselves *Dineh*, meaning "the people," and that they were a seminomadic people with a matrilineal society, so all property was passed down through the female line of a clan. Our clan was called *To'Adheedliinii*, which translates as "water flowing together" (hence the title for the documentary about me), and our relatives have always migrated between two homelands—one in the Chinle Valley area of the reservation and another at a higher elevation about ten or fifteen miles away. The oldest relative my mother could personally remember was my great-great-grandmother Ason Dijole, who lived to be 101 years old and whose name translates as "Round Woman" (an unfortunate name for the forebearer of a ballet dancer, I always thought). A tribal characteristic my mother had mentioned to me repeatedly—and on several occasions demonstrated quite dramatically with her own behavior—was that the Navajo are an extremely superstitious people.

Presumably my mother had recorded all of this family information and more on the computer that I had buried in solitary confinement in the back of my closet. But during those first few weeks after her death, whenever I thought about the laptop, I experienced a huge spasm of guilt, guilt laced with fear. I knew I should read whatever my mother had been writing, but I also felt that to do so would be like crossing a boundary between this world and the next—a reaction that, I suppose, exposes my own genetic Navajo susceptibility to superstition. I always feel a little awkward when I try to explain this, but for as long as I can remember I have been sensitive to the presence of spirits.

As a child I became aware of a particular ghostlike presence, a woman, who came into my room at night and stood near me, and sometimes even sat at the edge of my bed. When I complained to my mother about my uninvited visitor, she followed the advice of our family medicine man on the reservation and began administering sacred cornmeal—sprinkling it around the doors and windows of my room, and placing a little pinch of it under my tongue—to try to drive the ghost away. This often seemed to work for a while, but for years the ghost woman always came back. It was only when I was in my late thirties, in fact, after my mother arranged a ritual exorcism for me on the reservation, that I finally felt rid of the spirit who had been following me around for so many years. My ghost was finally gone, but now so was my mother. If I strayed across the boundary between this world and the next, whom might I encounter? And if some ghost began to stalk me again, who would help me this time?

On the day I finally worked up the nerve to pull my mother's laptop out of the closet, like any superstitious Navajo worth his salt, I was shaking with a bad case of nerves. As I pressed the power button and listened to the machine begin to whir and click, I began to hyperventilate. But half an hour later, after immersing myself in my mother's files, I felt calmer than I had in weeks. It was as if Mom's clear, strong voice was speaking to me again, and patiently explaining thoughts and feelings I had been wrestling with since her death, but had been unable to articulate for myself.

> One never really gets to know one's parents. I for one spent most of my life knowing I had parents, but not realizing their sacrifices, their worth and their love.

These were the opening sentences of a document titled "Mama Jo's History," in which Mom recounted her own early-childhood and teenage years. If my mother's opening words were true for most people, they were at least triply true for me. I had separated from my parents and started living on my own in New York at age fourteen.

Our parents try giving us a history of where we have come from. Do we listen? Of course not. It's only when we get to be our parents' age that all of a sudden we start asking why we are what we are.

With her next few sentences, Mom nailed me again. I always tried to listen when my mother talked about our family and our heritage, but the truth is, I also, on some level, always put invisible fingers in my ears. I was in voluntary exile. I had made the decision to leave the reservation and the life there long ago, and it made me feel nervous—and guilty—to be reminded of that life. As I began to read the files on my mother's laptop, my nervousness and guilt began to evaporate, and for the first time the world Mom had been trying to tell me about for so long suddenly began to come alive. I saw my great-great-grandmother Ason Dijole on one of her marathon walks, as my mother had often described her, striding across the desert with a walking stick in her hand, a colorful bandanna tied around her head, and her face rubbed red with a mixture of mutton tallow and ochre to protect it from the hot desert sun. I watched my grandma Rachel, whom I remembered as a quiet, stout old woman in velvet skirts, kick up her heels in the new persona of a fun-loving stand-up comic who was constantly laughing and cracking jokes. When she waxed the wooden floors of the elementary schoolhouse on the reservation, Grandma Rachel liked to play old 78 records on a hand-crank gramophone and dance and sing as she worked. After she had finished applying the wax, she would place her two little daughters—my mother and my aunt Alice—on a blanket and then whirl her delighted and squealing freight around the floor, "to bring out the shine."

My grandpa Bud also came to life, as a man of imposing stature with a lean face, long braided hair, and a tender heart. Admired for the enormous juicy tomatoes he grew in his carefully irrigated fields, Grandpa Bud was also famous as an accomplished drummer and singer who traveled throughout the West with his wife and their pack of little girls, performing Native songs and dances under the stage name of Laughing Boy. By the time my mother was four years old she was performing with my grandfather, using her own stage name of Redwing, dancing a number of ceremonial Native dances, but most notably the hoop dance—a ritual dance that traditionally was performed only by men and boys.

I was surprised to discover what a big role dancing had played in Mom's life. I knew that Grandpa Bud had taught her the hoop dance when she was very little, just as she later had taught it to me, and I knew that Mom—again, just like me—had performed at rodeos and Native American celebrations all around the West. But I was surprised to learn that my grandpa Bud also taught Mom the fox-trot and some waltzes, and the Charleston, and that he would partner her in performances of these at big barn dances. "Can you see my dad doing the Charleston?" Mom asks. "Navajo men didn't usually display that type of behavior. I believe he was way ahead of his time."

It was refreshing to learn that these relatives of mine, who always looked so distant and somber in all our family photographs, had actually had a little fun every now and then. And I was startled by how happy and fresh and innocent Mom's

early childhood sounded. She described weeks spent in the
wilderness herding sheep and goats, and long meandering
misadventures on horseback—in fact, every day seemed to
be taken by her as an opportunity for low-grade mischief and
spontaneous outdoor adventure.

By the time Mom started high school, however, shadows
started to fall across the jolly playing field of her youth. As a
teenager during the last part of the boarding school era for
Native Americans, when a federal policy of "assimilation"
made it mandatory for Indian children to attend government-
run schools that would impose Western traditions and "turn
Indians into Americans," Mom had to travel two hours to
Gallup, New Mexico, where she lived in a high school dormitory that housed children from all over the reservation.
During the summers she would return to her family, and to
a busy schedule of performing at powwows and rodeos—
but the back-and-forth was clearly confusing to her, and her
descriptions of life on the reservation grew less and less eu-
phoric. Her parents, she explains, had begun binge-drinking.
"When their checks came in the first of the month they could
be gone a couple of days or for a week at a time. I did not
enjoy going home for holidays, nor summer vacations. . . ."

By this time my vivacious but completely innocent mother
had begun to attract suitors, and in her amusing descriptions
of each she never fails to comment on his ability to dance.
Most didn't make the grade, but there was one tall, blond,
and blue-eyed young man named Jack—a highway construc-
tion worker from Colorado—who seemed to have come close.
Jack would show up at my grandparents' farm and literally
carry Mom out of the house to the car, and then drive her to

the middle of the reservation where they would turn up the car radio and dance the night away under the desert moon. "Boy, could Jack dance!" my mother comments. Jack loved watching my mother perform the hoop dance, and when she turned sixteen he offered my grandparents "five beautiful horses" for my mother's hand in marriage. "Of course my dad said no, because I was going to go to college," my mother writes.

That was always the plan, for my mother to go to college, and by the time she graduated from high school my mother had a definite idea of where she wanted to go. "I took the scholarship that took me farthest away from home," she says. In the summer of 1961, at age seventeen, she caught a train to Philadelphia, Pennsylvania, to attend nursing school. The trip to Philadelphia was the first train ride of her life and proved to be a miserable journey—she was sickened by all the cigarette smoke around her and bewildered when she had to change trains in Chicago. When she arrived in Philadelphia, she sat around the station for a long time, unsure of what to do next. When she finally called the school, whoever answered gave her the address and told her to catch a taxi. "I learned real fast that you do for yourself," Mom concludes.

This last phrase of Mom's haunted me after I read it. It had been under different circumstances, and to a very different place, but I too had decided at a young age to move far away from my home in the Arizona desert. And I too had learned real fast that you do for yourself. I thought of the feral and unchaperoned life I led as a young boy alone in New York, and then of my innocent and naive mother setting off to live on her own in Philadelphia at age seventeen—I'm sure the two of us were equally clueless when it came to sex or anything else that adult life might entail. The similarities between Mom's life and mine were comforting—we might not have had as much time together here on Earth as we would have liked, but we had a lot more in common than I had ever suspected. And though I had dreaded opening my mother's computer, I found that I loved hearing her voice again and cherished all the new images I now had of her when she was just a young girl. I felt I was learning much about her, and about myself at the same time. It reminded me of a comment my fellow NYCB dancer Lourdes Lopez once made after meeting Mom: "When you meet the mother," Lourdes said, "you understand the man."

When I compared my mother's early childhood and my own, I was struck by the strange circles of irony that can stack up in life. When my mother was a toddler, her father broke with tradition and taught his little daughter the Navajo hoop dance, a ritual that was traditionally performed only by men and boys. Grandpa Bud taught his little daughter a dance that was meant only for boys, and then years later Mom taught the dance to me—her little boy, who was in some ways more like a little girl. I was also struck by how my mother and I, though our lives had started on the same reservation and our experiences were only one slim generation apart, could have such different attitudes and responses to the world around us. I thought about an "encounter" with a snake I had had as a young boy one hot desert afternoon, when Kiko and I and my mother's brother and youngest sister, Orlando and Rochelle (Shelley), who were about our age, had hiked to a distant mesa where we liked to go whooping and sliding down the dusty, dry gullies. It was not much of an encounter really—in fact, the three of them simply mentioned to me that they had seen a snake along the way—but that was enough for me. I ran all the way home, screaming and laughing at the same time, tears streaming down my face at the thought of my close call.

But my mother had *real* encounters with rattlesnakes in the desert, and *she* never ran home screaming. Quite the contrary: "My mother prepared us for such encounters by tying a small pouch of an herb that is used to keep snakes at bay to the bottom of our skirts," she explains in one of her stories. Figuring they were protected from any possible harm, she and her sister Alice took turns jumping back and forth over a snake—"until we got tired or we tired the snake." I thought about how my mother used to send me pouches of magic healing herbs whenever I was injured as a dancer, and how I would dutifully tuck them into my backpack and carry them around with me everywhere. But try as I might, I couldn't imagine there existed a pouch of any substance that could ever, under any circumstances, have induced me to casually jump back and forth over a rattlesnake. Was this because I was a misfit as a Navajo from the very beginning—just not made of genuine Native American–brave material? Or was it because the traditional Native ways had fallen off so much by the time I grew up? I wasn't sure why, but reading my mother's stories about her childhood awakened feelings of regret and remorse at having "lost" my original culture—I felt haunted by a phantom way of life that was my road not taken.

For years I had heard people talking about the laws of circular motion as applied to dance, but as I looked backward

I seemed to be discovering the laws of circular motion as applied to family and life in general. I wanted to take all the new information I was gathering and break it down into beats, which is the language I understand best, to try to choreograph a kind of family hoop dance. But the more I tried to understand about my life and my family history the more I realized I didn't know. To fill in some of the holes I began to read—very tentatively—about various Native American traditions, and almost immediately I came across two ideas that fascinated me and helped me make sense of my situation. The first was the Native American belief in a circular, or "living," past, as opposed to the linear past of Western European tradition. For American Indians the past is never over; every "then" still exists in the "now"—it just exists on a different level. This made perfect sense to me as I thought about a dancer's constant challenge to show, with his or her body, how moments in time are linked, connected, and interactive—"We exist in time," as Mr. B had said. This concept of a "living past" was exciting to me because it implied that experience does not evaporate, so that if you miss the meaning of something the first time around, maybe you could go back and look again. In which case all those years that I had not spent with my family, as well as all the experiences I had enjoyed as a dancer with the NYCB, should all be—in some sense—still available for exploration.

The second Native American tradition that intrigued me was the intense physical and spiritual journey that Indian braves sometimes took, in search of their true self, called a vision quest. All my life I had been taught—by my mother and by my NYCB family—that I should try to move through life with truth and beauty and meaning. I realized that in order to do so now, given the recent changes in my life and the unknown topography of the future, I would need to embark on a vision quest through my living past, to try to see and feel all kinds of things I had not managed to see and feel before. If I could understand more about the steps I had or had not taken in my past, then maybe I would feel ready to choreograph my future.

The Sweet Confusion of a
Multicultural Identity Crisis

THERE HAVE BEEN times when I have found my multi-stranded heritage as a half Navajo, half Puerto Rican, All-American, dyed-in-the-wool New Yorker confusing. But as the years have passed I have become more comfortable with my unusual blend of family legacy and cultural experiences. I sometimes use cooking as a secret language, and at a small dinner party I recently hosted I decided to serve four different desserts: Navajo Fry Bread, Puerto Rican flan, American apple pie, and New York cheesecake. My guests were surprised by the bounty, but none of them guessed that there was a message in my madness.

My grandma Rachel taught my mother this recipe for Navajo Fry Bread, and my mother in turn taught it to my brother, Kiko, and me. Kiko became quite the expert Navajo-bread chef (and still is), and as young boys the two of us ran our own Fry Bread concession at various rodeos and pow-wows all over the Southwest. I would love to eat Fry Bread every day—but then I would be as big as a house.

Grandma Rachel's Navajo Fry Bread

SERVES 12

4 cups all-purpose flour
½ teaspoon salt
1 tablespoon baking
    powder

1½ cups lukewarm water
4 cups vegetable
    shortening or vegetable
    oil for frying

In a large bowl, combine the flour, salt, and baking powder. Add the lukewarm water slowly, kneading the mixture until it is soft but not sticky. Shape the dough into about 3-inch balls—you should have enough for 12 balls. On a floured surface, flatten the balls into patties and then roll them out to about ½-inch-thick circles.

On high (the surface of the oil should be shimmering but not smoking), heat the shortening in a large heavy skillet and fry the bread circles one at a time until nice and golden. Transfer the fried bread to a plate covered with a few paper towels. If you want to use the fried bread as a dessert, sprinkle the circles with powdered sugar and serve with honey. If you are going to eat the fried bread with chili or make a Navajo taco with meat sauce or beans with cheese, then salt the disks instead.

CHAPTER FOUR

Papa's Got a Brand-new Name

But the love of adventure was in Father's blood.
—WILLIAM FREDERICK "BUFFALO BILL" CODY

When my mother was alive, my father and I rarely had a telephone conversation that lasted longer than thirty seconds. He would always say, "Okay, Hon, well, here's Mom," and pass the phone to her. When I was very young and first living alone in New York I would get offended by this, not just because Pop seemed to have nothing to say to me, but also because he had called me "Hon." It was well-known in our family that before I was born my father had been hoping I would be a girl, and he always called my brother, Kiko, by the more manly nickname "Pop." I knew my father disapproved of gay men—as a child, before I even understood what he meant, I had heard him make fun of homosexuals by calling them "faggots"—but no one had ever talked to me about the issue of my own sexuality. (I know now that it must have been pretty obvious to others from early on that I was gay, even if not to me.) As I got older and more aware, I couldn't help resenting the disapproval, or at least the attitude, in the nickname my father had chosen for me. The desire to keep our telephone exchanges brief became mutual.

In the weeks immediately following Mom's death, however, my father and I began to call each other quite regularly, sometimes every day, and for the first time in our lives we even began to have some long talks. I was eager to connect with him on a new level and was full of questions as I explored my "living past," trying to fill in the blanks of my own and my parents' histories. He was lonely and at loose ends, traveling around the Southwest in his RV, trying to outrun the sadness that settled around him whenever he stopped moving. I never knew where he would be calling from, and in one of our late-night exchanges Pop announced that he had decided to go to Puerto Rico to visit his parents—my ninety-six-year-old grandmother and ninety-two-year-old grandfather—in their dilapidated hillside shack in a rural area of Puerto Rico. He said he needed to see them because there was a matter he had to put to rest. I had a hunch I knew what he was talking about, and it made me nervous.

My father has always believed that his father is not his biological father. For years he has told my brother and me that the tall green-eyed neighbor who lived next door to his parents looked like him—and that the big-eared, short person that his mother lives with, the supposed father whom he calls Don Lolo, did not. When I was growing up and during all my years dancing I never paid much attention to my father when he muttered these suspicions. But in my newly tender state as the motherless son of a widowed father, I found myself thinking about what it must have been like for Pop to carry such a painful doubt around inside him all his life. My father is a tall and handsome man, six foot one with a strong build and greenish eyes and thick white hair that was blond when he was younger. It is difficult to imagine anyone pushing him around, but he has told me and Kiko that Don Lolo used to beat him regularly when he was a little boy—sometimes with a belt, sometimes with a broomstick.

"He had a thick belt. He was a carpenter," Pop confirms when I ask him about this in one of our conversations. "Mom used to get in between Lolo and me when he started using his belt—she would be taking the shots for me." Finally a day came when my father was big enough and mad enough to grab the broomstick away from Don Lolo and threaten him back. "I was fourteen," he says, "but I was almost six feet tall already. Lolo was still five foot two." By that time Pop and his family had moved from Utuado, the small town in Puerto Rico where he was born and spent his first eight years, to Philadelphia, Pennsylvania. Already he had established a pattern of constant rambling.

"My dad hated my guts. I'd go anywhere not to be there," Pop says. At age fifteen my father lied and said he was seventeen so that he could join the air force for a three-year stint that kept him moving all over the United States in a nice agitated pattern. When his stint with the air force was over he wandered back to Puerto Rico for a while, where he took up with a woman named Lucy who was fifteen years his senior and the bartender at a local bar.

"We got sexually involved," no-nonsense Pop explains to me in his very faint Puerto Rican accent. I can almost hear him shrugging. "She gave me food and drink. I didn't have any money. It was very convenient." Lucy had two children from a previous marriage, and when she got pregnant they got married and moved with their baby—my half brother Mac Joe—from Puerto Rico to Philadelphia. That was in 1961. My father was twenty-two, and my mother, who was seventeen and just starting her nursing career, was also living in Philadelphia.

When Pop tells the story of how he and my mother started dating, despite the fact that he was married and had a young son, I hear him shrug again. "Puerto Rican men go out on their wives all the time. Same as the Cubans, same as the Mexicans," he explains. "They always have another woman. You know I cheated on your mother. A lot." Pop has taken to blurting out this last confession frequently ever since Mom has died—I don't know why—and hearing it always gives me a queasy feeling. As I get to know him better I am learning that my father has a roomy soul that can accommodate some very strange contradictions. Moments after declaring his numerous infidelities, he returns to the saga of how he and my mother met at a Puerto Rican salsa club in Philadelphia that he used to visit every Saturday when he took the night "off" from his wife, Lucy. Pop gets all sentimental and teary.

Mom was sitting in the corner with another girl from the nursing school when my father spotted her. "She was sitting there, her glasses were like Coke-bottle bottoms, they were so thick," Pop says. "I went over and asked her to dance, and she got up and danced with me. And I went away, but then I came back and we danced again and again, until she had to go home. I knew right away this was supposed to happen."

My mother was allowed to leave the nursing school only on Saturdays, provided her grades were good, so every Saturday for the next four weeks my father picked her up in his '49 Ford to take her out for the night. "She used to sit right next to the door," Pop says. "I told her, 'You know what? If I had a seat on the outside, you'd be out there.' Little by little I says, 'Come over here, sit next to me.' And little by little she did. Her grades were excellent—because she wanted to go out."

On the fourth Saturday my father announced to my mother that he was feeling restless, that he was going to leave Philadelphia and head out to California. "Do you want to come?" he asked her. Mom asked him for a week to think about it, and when he called the following Saturday she agreed to go. She had never had sex—in fact she didn't even know what sex was—and she headed off across the country with an older, married man she'd met only weeks before. "She quit school for me," Pop says, with a tremble in his voice. "She had a scholarship and everything. You know, love is funny—she quit school, and I just picked up and left my wife and baby."

My father may have had some trouble remembering he was married from time to time, but he has always had a bear-trap memory when it comes to anything about cars—which is why he can tell me that a friend who had a 1957 Pontiac four-door drove him and Mom across the country. They had a ham in a can and some bread and crackers—and not much else. Gas was twenty-five cents a gallon. When they got to Sacramento, they hung out in the park and ate at soup kitchens and stayed in flop joints where the rate was fifty cents per night per person. Pop would go up to the clerk to rent a room for one, and Mom would G.I. Joe–crawl past the desk so the clerk wouldn't see her. They had sex for the first time there in California, Pop tells me in one of his "overshare" moments. "Poor thing," my father says, shaking his head. "She was very, very naive." Not long after this they got the idea to stuff a pillow under Mom's shirt to make her look pregnant—as if this brilliant ruse was possible only now that they were having sex—and convinced a sympathetic banker to loan them three hundred dollars. "We ate for three days," remembers Pop.

When they had run through the last of their money, Mom called home and the two of them made their way to my grandparents' farm on the reservation. "I was not accepted," my father says bluntly. "I was not Navajo. They didn't like me. And I didn't want to stay." My father left the reservation and returned to Philadelphia by himself, but only two weeks later he came back to get my mother. This time the two of them left the reservation together, and by the time they returned, Mom was pregnant with my older brother, Kiko. When they got to my grandparents' home my grandpa Bud was waiting for them at the gate with a loaded shotgun in his hand. And it was not long after that my father got divorced from Lucy and he and my mother married. They settled into my grandparents' hogan on the reservation and on August 24, 1963, Kiko—whose full name is McKee Duane Soto—was born. A year and a half later, on April 16, 1965, I arrived.

Clearly my parents' first encounters and subsequent romance do not qualify as classic fairytale—or even Hollywood "meet-cute" material. In fact, I have never really let myself focus on several troubling details before—such as my mother's extreme innocence when she met my father and the fact that she scrapped her education to run off with a married man, and the existence of my half brother Mac Joe, who would have been just a baby when my father walked out on him and his mother. My father's casual attitude toward the marriage contract is another touchy issue that triggers painful memories that I have been reluctant to address over the years.

But despite all these less than perfect wrinkles, there is much about my humble family's humble beginnings that impresses me. Both of my parents went through some pretty rough times in their early years—much rougher, in fact, than anything I have had to endure. Both of them not only survived but in the process evolved into kind, decent, generous people. My father was brutally beaten as a child, but he grew beyond the awful example he was given. Pop never raised a hand against Kiko or me when we were young, and he always did his best to provide us with everything he could. My mother was practically a child herself when she started her family, and yet she was the most embracing, wise, and self-sacrificing mother anyone could ever want. She held us to high standards, but she was always there to help us meet them.

I was sitting at home alone, contemplating these stories about my family, one night when my father called and gave the family narrative a new twist. He was in Puerto Rico, visiting my grandparents, and he had had a very exciting day, he announced. After all these years he had finally extracted the truth from his mother, my grandma Margo. She had confirmed that Don Lolo was not his real father.

As soon as his mother admitted this to him, Pop and his brother Chico (who actually is Don Lolo's son, and has the short stature and big ears to prove it) had set off on a trip into the mountains to find the man who used to live next door to them. And they succeeded. Pop said it was amazing—the guy was six foot two, with my dad's same hair, same face, same green eyes. "Chico couldn't believe it—he looks exactly like me!" Pop crowed. "He's ninety-six now, but he's all put together. He looks real good." The man's name was Luis Cortez, and when Pop explained who he was and asked Mr. Cortez if perhaps he was his real father, the old man smiled and nodded.

It was touching how excited and happy my father sounded about all of this—almost proud. When I pointed out to him that this meant that technically he was a Cortez, not a Soto, he started laughing. Of course, this also means that we should all be named Cortez, not Soto—including my mother. As if I wasn't already confused enough about my identity. . . .

FOR YEARS I have struggled with a feeling of anxiety about falling between the cracks when it comes to the big traditional categories in life. On the reservation as a child I was a half Puerto Rican among pure Navajos; and on the reservation as a grown man I am an outsider from New York. As a teenager in New York I was a half Navajo, half Latino in the predominantly white world of Balanchine's ballets, and a neophyte in a high society of worldly sophisticates. But my confusion about my mix of cultures and heritages and life experiences, and the loneliness and feelings of displacement that have sometimes weighed me down over the years, seems to be growing less oppressive the more I learn. I suppose in an age when our forty-fourth president, Barack Hussein Obama, can casually refer to himself as a "mutt," we may even begin to find reasons to celebrate blended blood.

There have been moments in my dance career when people have pointed to my humble beginnings and saluted me as someone who has accomplished a great deal against great odds. This seems ludicrous to me now as I consider my mother and father and the unusual arc of their lives. It seems to me they accomplished much more against much greater odds. I have a new admiration for them, and I am beginning to understand how much I owe them. They may not have started with much, but they sure did their very best, and they sure gave me everything they could—which turns out to have been quite a lot.

A few months after he had discovered the truth about his own father, I invited my father to join me in Santa Fe for a weeklong stint I was doing as a guest teacher and choreographer for a modern dance troupe called Moving People Dance. It was the first time we had seen each other since Mom's death, and my goal was to take some of the sadness out of Pop's face. We stayed together at the apartment where my hosts were putting me up, in a community for retired gay people called Rainbow Vision. (Was there a hidden message here?) I cooked his favorite foods for him all week, and he drove me back and forth to my dance classes, the way he always used to when I was a kid. It almost felt like old times—although I did notice Pop had developed a new habit while driving, of reading signs out loud as he passed them. Once when he wasn't thinking, he automatically started driving us to the A-1 Storage facility where he and Mom used to live and work, instead of to our Rainbow Vision apartment. When I called him a homing pigeon, he said he was more like a faithful old dog that had been left downtown and was trying to find his way home.

Overall it was a quiet and healing week for both of us, and when my teaching duties were over we drove to Eagle Nest to see the house I had started building for Mom before she died. To distract us both from the sadness of Mom's absence I cooked a huge dinner featuring what I dubbed Enchiladas à la Cortez and told Pop the meal was in honor of his newfound biological father. He seemed pleased.

A little later he turned to me and asked me if I liked the way he had styled his hair. It was sort of curly looking, greased up with some new gel he had discovered. The question made me feel odd, as if I were somehow becoming a replacement for my mother. But I just nodded yes, and served him another helping of Enchiladas à la Cortez.

Later, as he was driving me to the airport, Pop turned to me again and said he was really proud of me and happy we'd spent this time together. I told him I felt the same way. It seems sad that it has taken until Pop is in his seventies and I am in my midforties for us to begin to trust in our love for each other—but then, I tell myself, when it comes to finding fathers, better late than never.

In Celebration of Finding Fathers

ONE OF MY father's favorite meals, one I often make when I am visiting him out west, is an enchilada dish my mother taught me. After Pop made his fateful trip to Puerto Rico and went digging for his "roots," I renamed the dish Enchiladas à la Cortez—in honor of my father's finding his real father. Originally this recipe involved frying the tortillas first and then rolling them into enchiladas. I always love a shortcut, so I decided to save time (and calories) by skipping the frying and rolling steps, and instead layering the tortillas with the meat sauce to make a casserole. I love this easier version of the traditional recipe—and so does my father, José Anthony Soto à la Cortez.

Enchiladas à la Cortez

SERVES 8

2 tablespoons vegetable oil
3 pounds ground sirloin
1 large onion, chopped
2 jalapeño peppers, diced
4 10-ounce cans enchilada sauce

1 10¾-ounce can condensed cream of mushroom soup
Salt and pepper
6 cups grated cheddar cheese
24 6-inch corn tortillas

Get a large skillet nice and hot. Add the vegetable oil and then add the ground sirloin. Brown the meat for 5 minutes. Add the onion and jalapeños, and cook for about 5 minutes over high heat. Add the enchilada sauce and the cream of mushroom soup, and add salt and pepper to taste; simmer gently for about 20 minutes, covered.

During this time you can shred your cheese—or to make life easier you could just buy shredded cheese—and preheat the oven to 375 degrees.

When your meat sauce is ready, turn off the heat and prepare your assembly line. Ladle a cup of sauce onto the bottom of a large casserole dish. Layer tortillas to cover the sauce and add a layer of cheese. Repeat the sauce-tortilla-cheese layering, ending with sauce and cheese.

Cover the casserole dish tightly with aluminum foil and bake for 30 minutes. Then remove the foil and bake for another 10 to 15 minutes, so that the cheese gets bubbly and a little golden brown—but not burned.

Remove the casserole from the oven and let it sit for about 10 minutes before serving with white rice—and a salad if you like.

CHAPTER FIVE

Saturday Nights and Sunday Picnics in Paradise Valley

*The turning point in the process of growing
up is when you discover the core of strength within
you that survives all hurt.*

—MAX LERNER

I n the documentary about me, my mother says, "Jock was dancing in my tummy, before he was even born." After reading her account of my birth I realize that her remark may have been a polite reference to the week of contractions and four days of painful labor she endured before I finally arrived in the Indian Medical Center in Gallup, New Mexico, one hundred miles from the reservation where she and my father were living. Mom and Pop picked my first name from a pamphlet of names ("of Hebrew origin," my mother notes rather oddly) that was lying around the hospital, and decided that my father's middle name could do double duty as a middle name for me. "Jock Anthony Soto. Who, at the time, would have imagined his destiny?" my proud mother writes as she describes my birth.

At the time, my mother was working as a secretary for the principal at the Lukachukai Boarding School on the Navajo Reservation and my father had a job driving trucks, and they were living in the octagonal hogan on my grandfather's land. Sometime after my birth my parents started a small Laundromat on the reservation, but apparently this venture was short-lived. "Joe and Jo have always been travelers," my mother writes breezily as she launches into a dizzying description of the year after my birth, during which she and my father yo-yoed from Chinle, Arizona (where they were living with my mother's parents), to Philadelphia (to live with my father's parents), to Utuado, Puerto Rico (to live near my father's grandparents), then back to Philadelphia for a while, and finally back to Arizona, where they "settled." My mother got a job with the local telephone company and my father worked loading and transporting cotton, and Kiko and I were entrusted to a woman named Zita—the first in a series of Spanish-speaking babysitters who watched us while our parents worked. "Zita's grandson taught Kiko how to do the 'Monkey' and he entertained us with the new dance all evening," my mother writes. "Jock came home talking gibberish, thinking he was talking Spanish."

When I think back to these earliest years of my life I have a difficult time pulling up clear images of the various houses and apartments we inhabited. I remember a living room with a brick mantelpiece, on which I split my head open when Kiko pushed me during a game we had invented called "Vampire," and a spacious kitchen where in the evenings my mother and father would play their salsa and merengue music and dance. I remember our dogs—a dachshund named Heidi (who got run over and killed), a beagle named Freckles, and a boxer named Pebbles (so named for his odd habit of gobbling small stones). But my most abiding sense of these early years is one of *constant movement*. We were a restless little family, always packing up and heading somewhere. We made frequent trips back to the reservation to spend time with our relatives, and we traveled a seasonal circuit of rodeos and powwows, where I would perform the hoop dance and we would set up our family's concession booths. Kiko and I would cook and sell Navajo Fry Bread and Navajo tacos alongside my parents, who sold the kachina dolls and painted pottery that Mom had made. Kiko was always a favorite with our customers, because he was so handsome and flirty. I loved to watch him as he won the girls over.

In her later years my mother sometimes would try to make the case that our constant movement as a family was owing to the fact that historically the Navajo have always been a no-madic tribe—but of course Mom was the only full-blooded Navajo among us. Whatever their reasons, my parents did shift back and forth between the reservation and various homes in the Phoenix area in the early years of my life, and this section of my mother's "family history" reads like a cata-log of local addresses. It was in the fourth or fifth of these homes, a little brick house on Ninth Street in Phoenix, while watching *The Ed Sullivan Show* on an old black-and-white television, that I saw my first ballet. The segment featured the amazing Edward Villella dancing the "Rubies" movement of Balanchine's *Jewels*.

"It surprised Mama Jo that both Kiko and Jock were en-thralled by the performance," writes my mother, referring to herself in the third person as she so often did. "They both went to bed immediately after; however, the next morning Jock came to Mama Jo and said, 'That's what I want to do.' Mama Jo asked, 'What are you talking about?' and Jock described the ballet, mimicking the leaps and jumps of the dancers he had seen. He was about four and a half at the time."

Whenever I try to return to that pivotal moment when I was watching *Ed Sullivan*, what I remember most is feeling spellbound by what a real *guy* Villella was, and being fascinated by the virility he projected while dancing so magnificently. It amazed me that these two qualities—supreme maleness and beautiful movement—could be combined to make something so powerful. What now strikes me as equally amazing as I think about the famous family anecdote is the fact that my mother and father took their four-year-old son's request seriously and immediately set about finding a ballet school. "What would it be like to have a little Indian-slash-Spanish boy dance ballet?" my mother remembers asking a Ms. Timona Pittman at the Phoenix Children's Workshop. "Who?" Ms. Pittman asked. "How old is he? Ballet boys are hard to find." A minute later Ms. Pittman was on the phone arranging an audition for me at the Phoenix School of Ballet.

I will never forget my first visit to this ballet school, run by the talented Kelly and Isabel Brown, and my first sight of the old studio with its wooden floors. My father had been entrusted with the chore of shopping for my audition outfit, and he had grabbed whatever he could find to improvise his notion of a ballet costume. When I arrived I was dressed in little shorts, a white T-shirt, and blue fishnet stockings—the closest thing he could find to tights. My parents and my brother had all come with me, and they watched as Kelly took me to the front of the class and showed me different positions, stretching my arms and legs this way and that. Kelly impressed me with his animated and happy presence, and the way he demonstrated everything with an exaggerated style. It was fun to try to copy his movements. And I *loved* the music that Kelly played for us, starting and stopping it as needed by lifting and lowering the needle on a record player in the corner of the room. I had never heard anything like it before. I knew right away that I wanted to come back to that studio as often as possible.

"Of course, as parents, Mama Jo and Papa Joe were the nervous ones," my mother writes of the moment when she watched her fishnet-stockinged son enter a ballet studio for the first time. "We watched Jock enter—no fear. Kelly put Jock up front where he could keep an eye on him, and during class he took the time to correct his positions, stretching Jock's limbs and working with him for an hour." After class, Kelly came out and told my parents that he expected me for classes every week, and that he was putting me on a full scholarship. I was the only boy ballet student at the school. "Jock quickly left his classmates behind," my proud mother claims. "Choreography, he picked up on one walk-through, and he was doing pirouettes perfectly without a pause by the age of 8 or 9. Kelly choreographed several ballets for him, which he performed in and around Phoenix and Tucson. Mama Jo and Papa Joe could hardly keep up with the tights, shoes and gasoline."

. . . .

IT OCCURS TO me now that the six years when I was a student at the Phoenix School of Ballet were probably the longest and most stable stretch my parents and my brother and I ever had together as a family. Maybe my classes with Kelly and Isabel Brown, and my parents' commitment to help me pursue my newfound passion for ballet, helped anchor us a little—or at least contained our wanderings to a smaller area. Not long after I began attending ballet classes my parents decided to move from our little brick house in Phoenix to a new housing development called Paradise Valley that had been plunked down in the desert outside Scottsdale. Paradise Valley was a considerable distance from downtown Phoenix, and it had the eerie look of the community from the movie *Poltergeist* in that five different house designs were repeated over and over—so you see your house, then four more houses, and then your exact house again every five houses, over and over all the way down the street. We had a garage and a carport and a fenced backyard, where my parents optimistically planted grapevines. We all had water beds in our bedrooms (mine used to undulate ominously whenever the ghost woman came to visit me at night) and an assigned seat at the kitchen table. It definitely felt like we were coming up in the world, and it even seemed possible that we might stay put for a while.

Unfortunately the commute from Paradise Valley to my ballet school was brutal—almost two hours each way, and usually it was my father who drove me. This was the beginning of a long commuting relationship between the two of us—he would always drive, and I would always ride—that has persisted to this day. Long stretches of travel together in a car can do odd things to two people—it's as if over time all kinds of unspoken feelings take shape and ride along like additional passengers. I cannot count the number of hours of my life that I have spent alone in a car with my father, and it makes me wince now to think how many of those hours in my youth—and especially my adolescence—were spent in complete and somewhat hostile silence.

Paradise Valley had all the trappings of a typical suburban community, but it was surrounded by empty, wild desert where there were rolling tumbleweeds and wandering herds of horses and the eerie howl of the coyote echoing through the darkness every night. Nature performed herself dramatically in this desertscape, serving up sudden dust storms and flash floods that seemed to come from nowhere and immense dark rain clouds laced with fierce bolts of lightning that you could watch advancing from miles and miles away. In the summer, temperatures would get up to more than 120 degrees during the day, and you didn't dare venture outside your house until well after sundown, when things had cooled a little. I can remember strapping on my roller skates after dinner. I would play the compilations of classical music that my father picked up for me at swap meets on an old record player in our garage, and skate around the carport, practicing my ballet moves in the pale moonlight. (My poor brother, Kiko, would often hide inside during such exhibitions.)

When we first moved to Paradise Valley, Kiko and I were enrolled at Arrowhead Elementary, and every afternoon Kiko would take me by the hand and walk me either home or to our babysitter Hortensia's house if we were supposed to spend our afternoon there. My loyal brother walked me home from elementary school every single day, and in later years, when the word got out that I was dancing ballet, he became my protector, sticking up for me when the other kids teased me. I worshipped Kiko—he was the ultimate older brother, strong and handsome and hugely popular at school. I watched with awe as he navigated a social world that was completely mysterious to me. Looking back, I realize that my brother was a *stud*—tall, athletic, and very muscular, with naturally wavy hair. (He didn't have to ask my mother to feather his hair!) All the girls were chasing him, and I was vaguely curious about what he must be doing when he sometimes brought one of them home and disappeared into his room for long periods of time.

There was one of Kiko's girlfriends whom I was particularly fond of, because she would arrive on horseback and leave her horse tied in the yard while she and Kiko were in Kiko's bedroom doing God only knows what for hours. While she and Kiko were locked away, I would slip the horse from its halter and climb onto its back and go galloping out across the desert. The horse was very well trained, and I would ride it bareback, steering with its mane. I would race back and forth across the desert—I loved going really fast—and then ride back home and quietly tie up the horse again on our lawn. This is one of several memories that seems almost surreal to me now. I wouldn't dream of climbing on a horse these days—in fact, I can't even walk past a horse without thinking it might bite me with its big old teeth or kick me with a back hoof and break my shin. For years while I was dancing with the NYCB I had to avoid potentially dangerous sports like skiing and riding, and somehow, over time, I have convinced myself that I am terrified of horses. But back then, galloping bareback across the desert seemed the most natural thing in the world. It was completely exhilarating. It was freedom.

During those years when I was watching with great curiosity as Kiko juggled his various girlfriends, I never felt the slightest urge for physical interaction with girls myself. Of course, I was still young and probably not feeling definite sexual urges of any kind. But I do remember being fascinated by our babysitter Hortensia's teenage son when he sat and watched television with us. On hot days, when he took off his shirt, my jaw dropped as I stared at his bare chest and shoulders. I remember sitting near him on the sofa and slowly stretching out the ears and legs of my very large talking Bugs Bunny to make Bugs take up more and more of the empty sofa on my right side, so that I could inch closer and closer to the hunky teenager seated on the sofa to my left. I was only seven or eight at the time, but obviously on some level I already knew I was gay.

Another memory that would support this theory floated back to me recently. It took place on an afternoon when Pop and Kiko weren't around, and I was sitting on the couch in our living room in Paradise Valley, watching Mom vacuum. Mom was in her early thirties, and for some reason she was wearing a blond wig. Maybe my dad had brought it home for her. I'm not sure why she was wearing the wig, but the blond hair looked very strange against the color of her skin. I was dying to try the wig on myself, to see how I would look with blond hair. (Exactly like my mother, is the answer.) At the time I was obsessed with the movie *Funny Girl* starring

Barbra Streisand, and as soon as Mom removed her wig and set it aside, I grabbed it and disappeared into Kiko's and my bedroom. I made a bikini top with one towel and used two more towels to create a bustle in the rear and settled the blond wig onto my head. Holding a brush as a microphone, I played the sound track from *Funny Girl* on the record player, stood in front of the mirror, and began lip-synching to the song "People," doing my best to imitate Ms. Streisand's movements and facial expressions. Halfway through my performance, the bedroom door slowly opened, revealing my father's astonished face. I stopped and stared back at him, just as speechless as he was, blushing to my toes. Not a word was said as he slowly closed the door again. The only sound that could be heard was Ms. Streisand's voice singing " . . . are the luckiest people—in the world!"

Even in these early years it must have occurred to my parents that I might be gay—but this was not something we talked about then, or for years to come. I have never sensed the slightest disapproval about my sexuality from my mother's side of the family, and just recently I learned that in the Navajo culture being gay is considered a special quality, indicating that a person is more evolved spiritually than others. Clearly the same is not true in the Puerto Rican culture of my father's heritage. I sensed intense, if unspoken, disapproval from my father about my sexuality when I was growing up. As recently as 2005, when my parents and I visited my Puerto Rican grandparents in their shack in the middle of the slums of Puerto Rico, as part of our research for *Water Flowing Together*, I was shocked to discover that Pop had never told Grandma Margo and Don Lolo that I was gay. It was the first time they had seen me since I was a young kid, and they kept asking me why I didn't have a family yet. I kept waiting for Pop to explain—but he never said a thing.

Another topic that was never discussed in our house during my Paradise Valley years was where my father disappeared to every Saturday night. Almost every week during the years when I was ages five to ten, in the late afternoon or early evening on Saturdays, my father would start his weekly ritual. He would shower and shave and put on his nicest clothes, whistling and singing all the while, and then dab a little fragrant cologne on his cheeks. Throughout these ablutions my mother and Kiko and I would snuggle together on the sofa, watching Pop get himself all snappy, and getting ready for our own evening of watching television together. Sometimes, after he had dressed but before putting his shoes and socks on, my father would call my mother over and she would kneel down and clip his toenails for him. When he was all dressed and groomed, Pop would say good-bye and leave. This was the ritual every weekend, and to Kiko and me it seemed to be a pretty happy ritual, especially since every Sunday when Pop came home again we would all pile into his 1965 white Cadillac convertible with the ruby-red interior and go on a big family picnic. We would head out into the desert with the top down and the wind blowing through our hair. Kiko and I would sip Cokes in the backseat and sing along to the Eagles at top volume when it was our turn to pick the music, while Mom and Pop drank their tomato-juice-and-beer in the front seat. Pop would salsa dance with the steering wheel when it was his turn; Mom, seated beside him and wearing her trademark scarf and wide-brimmed hat and oversize sunglasses, resembled a Native American Audrey Hepburn. We would cruise across the hot desert toward Oak Creek Canyon, where we would pick a roadside picnic spot at random—it didn't really matter where we stopped. The point was the four of us were all there together, on a Sunday family picnic adventure.

As far as I knew, every pop in Arizona left home on Saturday night and then came home on Sunday to take his family on a splendid picnic. At the time it would never have occurred to me that my father was going to spend the night with another woman, and even now, as I write this I can't understand how my mother could abide such behavior for as many years as she did. The whole situation came to an ugly head one Christmas Day when I was ten. Kiko and I were out riding our bicycles around Paradise Valley when we saw our father's Cadillac cruising toward us. Everyone in our neighborhood knew his car—Pop was so proud of it, and we were always proud, too, whenever he drove up in it to pick us up from school. Now he was approaching us in his fabulous car, and as he came to a stop we peered inside.

"Say hello to your brother Charles," my father said as he pointed to a little boy sitting next to him. Kiko and I looked at each other. We both knew about our half brother Mac Joe from Philadelphia, because he had come to stay with us briefly a few years earlier. He was a strange boy who one day during his visit had wrapped his arms around me and sucked on my neck in order, I now understand, to give me a hickey. But the boy in the car was not Mac Joe. "That's not our brother," I said, shaking my head in disbelief. And then Pop took off, heading for our house.

Kiko and I sped home as fast as we could on our bikes, and got there just in time to see Pop and the boy called Charles getting back into the car. It had been only a couple of minutes. As they drove off, we ran in to find our mother, but she wasn't in the house. We started racing around the neighborhood, shouting her name, desperate to find her. After searching and searching, we finally found Mom. She was sitting, crying, in an empty canal that handled the overflow from flash floods and heavy rains.

"How could he do this?" she asked. "How could he do this to me?" I felt like someone had put a knife right through me—I couldn't stand to see my mother cry. Eventually Kiko and I calmed Mom down. We hugged her and we talked to her and we took her home. I was too young to understand exactly what had happened. But as I fell asleep that night there was one thing I knew for sure: my father had hurt my mother. He had made her cry. And I was furious with him, and with the little Christmas-surprise boy named Charles.

Charles was about five when my father brought him home to meet us that Christmas, and he did not visit our Paradise Valley home ever again. I suppose Mom and Pop must have worked something out. I have a vague memory that Mom said she was going to take Kiko and me and divorce Pop—and that then Pop realized he couldn't live without my mother, so he stopped seeing the other woman. This seems a plausible enough script, whether or not it actually happened.

As I write this I am haunted by the vision of my mother kneeling to trim my father's toenails so that he can go spend the night with another woman. But I am also haunted by a scene that occurred not so many years ago, when I flew out to visit my parents in Gallup, New Mexico. Kiko had picked me up at the airport, and as we were driving to the trailer off Route 66 where Mom and Pop were living at the time, he turned to me and asked if Mom had warned me that Charles—the little Christmas-surprise boy—would be at the trailer. She had not. I was incredulous, but sure enough when we got to the trailer, there he was. My reaction was not particularly nice. When Kiko got out of our car I stayed put and rolled up all the windows and locked all the doors. I was a grown man, and so was Charles—but I acted as if I were still a ten-year-old boy who was furious at a five-year-old boy who had arrived unannounced on Christmas Day and made his mother cry.

My father and Kiko and Charles were all skulking around outside the trailer, glancing at me nervously. They knew I was upset. My mother was waving to me, gesturing for me to get out of the car. I wouldn't budge. She walked over and knocked on the window and asked me to roll it down. At first I resisted, but when I finally opened the window I looked Mom in the eye and asked her how she could stand this. Mom looked right back at me and said, "All has been forgiven, Jock. He's part of the family now." I stared at her in disbelief. Then I followed her into the trailer, still furious but thinking that my mother must be the strongest woman in the world, and a saint.

As it turned out, Charles had been living with my parents in their trailer that year, at my mother's insistence. My mother had forgiven my father and had accepted Charles into her home with the same warm and loving embrace she extended to everyone, because it would have offended her ideals of harmony and humanity to do anything else. I could not summon the same largesse of spirit within myself at the time, but even from beyond the grave Mom continues to teach me things—the same way she said she herself was always taught as a young girl on the reservation: by example. New lessons come from her all the time, and over the last few years I have come to understand that Mom is right about Charles. He *is* part of our family, and family is one of the most important things in life. These days when I consider Charles's situation, I feel sorry for him. Truly, none of this was his fault. I have always had a father, flawed as he may be, and so has my brother, Kiko. Poor Charles never really had a father. Since my mother passed away Kiko and I have been making a greater effort to keep in touch with our half brother Charles, and he often joins us when we get together with my—and his—father. I know Mom, wherever she is, must be watching and smiling, wondering what she should teach us next.

The Happy Family Picnic

ON SUNDAY MORNINGS when I was young my mother would get up early, carefully apply her makeup, and then head to the kitchen to put together our family picnic. The menu varied, but my favorite entrées were always chicken-cheese-alfalfa-sprout sandwiches (on white bread with tons of mayonnaise) and Mom's special "barbecued" chicken, which she actually cooked in a casserole in the oven. The chicken can also be "barbecued" on the stovetop or in a Crock-Pot if you don't have an oven.

One of the wonderful things about picnics is they will work just about anywhere. You need only transport a tasty meal to a place where you don't normally eat—it could be your living room floor—and the rest is all attitude. For my brother, Kiko, and me, sitting in the backseat of my father's 1965 Cadillac convertible with the top down and the wind blowing through our hair on our way to a family picnic was about as good as life got.

Mom's Stove-Top BBQ Chicken

SERVES 10

8 chicken thighs, bone in,
   with skin
8 chicken legs, bone in,
   with skin
2 whole chicken breasts,
   bone in, with skin,
   each breast halved and
   quartered

1 large Spanish onion,
   finely chopped
¾ cup chicken broth
Salt and pepper
3 cups honey-mustard
   barbecue sauce

Heat the oven to 350 degrees.

Place the chicken and onions in a large casserole dish, and pour in the broth. Add salt and pepper to taste. Mix these with your hands until everything is coated.

Cover the casserole dish with aluminum foil, and place in the oven to bake. After 45 minutes, add the barbecue sauce and toss to coat the chicken evenly. Turn the oven up to 475 degrees, and bake without the foil for another 10 to 15 minutes, or until the chicken starts to dry a bit. Keep an eye on it to prevent it from drying too much—every oven is different. Remove from the oven and cool for 10 minutes, covered loosely with foil, before serving.

This is delicious served hot, lukewarm, or cold—but make sure you have plenty of napkins.

CHAPTER SIX

Losing Arizona

Make something beautiful of your life.
—ABRAHAM VERGHESE, *CUTTING FOR STONE*

By the time I was nine or ten the world of ballet at large and my own weekly ballet classes had become an alternate reality for me, a place where I could hide and dream. I still acted out my role as just another neighborhood kid in the desert community where I lived, but I also lived another, more exciting, life inside the small studio of the Phoenix School of Ballet. I was attending more and more classes, which meant spending more time waiting to be picked up. I can remember spending much of that idle time locked in the school's one and only dressing room, where I would try on various items from the lost-and-found bin and dance all around in the borrowed outfits, becoming different characters. When people came banging on the door—"Let us in! We need to change!"—I would quickly strip and get back in my own clothes and open the door and exit as nonchalantly as possible.

Stories of a bigger ballet world beyond my little Arizona

school drifted back to me and I hoarded every detail and dreamed of becoming part of that world someday. Three of Isabel and Kelly's children—Leslie, Ethan, and Elizabeth—were studying ballet in New York, and there was huge excitement in our school when rumors surfaced that Leslie might be cast in a film, dancing with Mikhail Baryshnikov, who had recently defected from Russia. (She did get the part, and in fact was nominated for an Oscar for her role in *The Turning Point*, a film I must have watched a hundred times in the year or so after it came out.) I had seen news coverage and clips of Baryshnikov on the television, and I wanted desperately to get an autographed picture of him. My mother found out where to send mail for Baryshnikov so that I could write a letter to him—and he actually sent me an autographed picture all the way to Arizona. (I still have that autographed photo, but I have never told Misha about it. When he and I see each other these days he says, "Hi, old man," and I say, "Hi, older man.")

During my studies at his ballet school, Kelly Brown had choreographed some short pieces for me, and when I was eleven he decided to choreograph the annual Christmas show for me and a little girl from the school. The ballet started with the two of us sleeping. (I think Kelly was trying to make a little *Nutcracker*-type thing without copying it.) When we awoke, there was Santa Claus, and a whole flurry of little dancing tree ornaments. The show ended up getting some attention, and an article in the local newspaper described me as "an eleven-year-old phenomenon." Well, I was one of a handful of boys dancing in Arizona—so of course they thought I was a phenomenon! The buzz brought the local TV station in to do a little story—and that was the end of my reputation.

When I walked into my homeroom at school the next morning, there on the chalkboard, in huge block letters, were the words JOCK IS A SISSY. I read them, and then—like any good sissy—I turned around and ran all the way home, crying. Children can be so cruel, and from then on my schoolmates teased me mercilessly, calling me "Ballet-Sissy" and "Gay Boy." Kiko did his best to protect me, but the news about my ballet studies—which my parents had deliberately tried to keep under wraps—was out. In a defensive strategy, I made friends with the only African American girl at our school, who was also getting picked on a lot, and another little boy who was unpopular. We three losers hung out together and tried to protect one another.

That was the unfortunate fallout from my Christmas performance. A happier result came when a talent scout saw the performance and was impressed by what she considered to be my natural abilities and stage presence. She came backstage and took my parents aside and told them that I should go to New York City and audition for the School of American Ballet and work with George Balanchine. Once again my mother took my ballet future seriously enough to follow through—in fact the next day she called SAB and set up an audition for me. At the time I had never heard of the New York City Ballet, and I had no idea who George Balanchine was. The American Ballet Theatre was the dance company that seemed to always be in the press in those days, and I just assumed that the School of American Ballet must be their school. But none of these details mattered to me—I was excited beyond belief when my mother announced that she and my father had scraped together some money and

that she and I were going to fly to New York, where I would
be auditioning at a new ballet school.

I never thought twice about the fact that my father would
not be coming with us to New York for the audition—not just
because we couldn't afford another plane ticket, but also because my father had always taken a neutral, backseat position
when it came to my pursuit of dance. (I had been aware for
some time that it embarrassed him slightly to have a "sissy"
ballet son.) He was happy to let my mother handle all the
logistics of my ballet career, in part because he had projects
of his own he was trying to launch in the world of art and
entertainment. Pop had always been intrigued by the entertainment industry (I think he secretly longed for his own talk
show, a Merv Griffin kind of thing) and several years earlier
he had decided to try his hand as a part-time talent agent for
Native American performers. At about the same time that I
was offered an audition at the SAB, Kiko was emerging as
one of the rising stars in my father's rather small stable of
talents. Kiko had auditioned for and landed some good parts
as an actor, and everyone was excited about his prospects.
It seemed the most natural thing in the world to me that my
mother would shepherd me in my dance pursuits, while my
father accompanied Kiko in his acting efforts. It was a divide-
and-conquer division of duty that suited me, especially given
the tense relationship between my father and me.

I WILL NEVER forget that first visit to New York City. It
was overwhelming and at the same time exhilarating. I was
stunned by the tall buildings and millions of people rushing

everywhere, the thousands of cars jamming the streets, the labyrinthine underground world of the subways. I had grown up in the wide-open desert, where we rode horses through miles of emptiness and listened to the lonely coyote opera at night. I lived in an empty, dry frying pan of hot sand, where rattlesnakes liked to cool themselves in the puddles of oil that leaked from our car onto the driveway. I had never experienced anything like the crazy, bustling energy that electrified the streets of New York—but the instant I encountered it I loved it.

The School of American Ballet was located in the Juilliard School building at that time, and I remember as we walked through Juilliard, following the signs for SAB, I felt like Alice in Wonderland. The doors looked so tall. Everything looked so fancy and grand and official. When we reached the school itself I was stunned by the glimpses I caught of huge studios with polished floors and real pianos. My school in Phoenix was in a strip mall and had one small studio with an old record player in the corner.

When we found the office for the school, two Russian ladies, as angular and exotic as rare birds, greeted us. One was Natasha Gleboff, the director of the school, and the other was a teacher at the school, Mme Tumkovsky. Together they took me into one of the studios and began the auditioning procedure. Mme Tumkovsky grabbed my foot and talked in Russian to Natasha—probably saying, "He's got bad feet"—while Natasha wrote down notes. I was somewhat terrified, but I just let them go about their business. Tumkovsky took my leg and checked my extension—more notes. She put me through a very short barre session, and then it was to the center. I believe it was when she asked me to do pirouettes that I won them over—I could do multiple turns. When the audition was over they offered me a full scholarship and a place in the intermediate boys' class, starting the very next day if I wanted. I was in shock.

After the audition, while my mother was in the office, filling out some forms, I looked around my new school with hungry eyes. I noticed a very tall white-haired man lurking in the hallways—he looked important. His arms were crossed behind his back and he was a little hunched over, with his chin sticking forward in a somewhat menacing way. I was convinced this must be Balanchine. When my mother came out, this man approached us and pointed his finger at me and said, "Good audition." Then he asked if we would like to see a class. We said yes, and he took us into a studio where we sat and watched. That was going to be me, I kept thinking as I stared. I would be dancing alongside these other boys. It wasn't until much later that I discovered that the tall white-haired man was not Balanchine. He was Lincoln Kirstein, the man who first brought Mr. B to America to start a ballet school, and then later to start the New York City Ballet—the company that would become my surrogate home and would for thirty years remain the platform for the pursuit of my all-consuming dream.

EVERYTHING HAPPENED SO quickly. The SAB offered me a full scholarship, my parents accepted the offer, and the following fall my mother and I moved to New York. One, two, three, just like that. In retrospect it is stunning to me how promptly and completely my parents rearranged their lives to support my passion for ballet. There were no dormitory facilities at SAB at the time, so students had to find their own housing. As it happened, my father's cousin "Aunt G" lived in the Bronx, and Mom and I moved in with her practically overnight. This all seemed to me to be the obvious course of action back then, but as I think about it now I realize that it was really a remarkable response on my mother's part. She made a snap decision to separate herself from my father and Kiko, both of whom were going to stay out west. When I pause now and put together pieces of our family history that I never bothered to examine before, I can't help wondering if my mother's impulsive decision to move to New York City could have had anything to do with the appearance of a little boy named Charles the previous Christmas. Perhaps my mother and father needed some breathing space, some time to figure things out. Whether or not this was the case, something was working in my favor. I had been presented with an extraordinary opportunity, and my mother and father had made decisions—decisions that involved sacrifices—to ensure that I could grab that opportunity. I was one lucky little Navajo-Puerto-Rican-gay-would-be-ballet-dancer.

I was twelve years old when my mother and I moved to New York in the fall of 1977, and I immediately fell in love with every aspect of the city. I was in heaven—I never wanted to leave. But as luck would have it, my first thrilling taste of life as a student at the SAB was to be sadly short-lived. My poor mother had scrambled to move us into Aunt G's one-bedroom apartment in the Bronx and to enroll me in the sixth grade at a local parochial school, and every afternoon we made the hideous subway commute to Lincoln Center for my ballet classes. But after only two months I developed such severe growing pains behind both knees that I had to stop dancing and withdraw from the school.

My memories surrounding this disastrous development in my life are strange and sparse. I remember the electric thrill of living in New York and studying at Balanchine's school, and the thudding boredom of my sixth-grade classroom and schoolwork. I remember the amused outrage I suffered every time I went grocery shopping with Aunt G, because of the way she would grab a big old bag of chips off the shelf and eat them as we wandered the aisles, crumpling and tossing the empty bag aside without ever paying for the chips. And that's about it. I simmered along in my early-adolescent stew of excitement and boredom and humiliation—and then as suddenly as it had begun, my New York adventure was over.

At about the same time that Mom and I had moved to New York to pursue my ballet dreams, my father and Kiko had moved to Los Angeles to pursue Kiko's acting opportunities. (I know my mother and father sound like such stage parents, but they really were not.) When I had to withdraw from the SAB, Mom and I left New York and headed west to join Pop and Kiko in California. My father had a job managing an apartment building in the Van Nuys section of the San Fernando Valley, and we lived in an apartment on the first floor of the building.

When Mom and I got out there, Kiko's acting career really seemed to be taking off—he had landed the lead in a film called *Three Warriors* that was being made by Saul Zaentz, the producer who had won an Oscar for Best Picture for *One Flew over the Cuckoo's Nest*. Acting under his real first name of McKee and the stage surname of Redwing (Mom's Native American nickname), Kiko played a Sioux Indian boy named Michael, whose father died when he was very young, and who left the reservation with his mother to go live in the big city. I had to laugh recently when I read a description of this film and Kiko's role as "a troublesome teenager who has a problem shaping his identity and denies his Native American heritage"—how life imitates art! But when my fourteen-year-old big brother was in production for his exciting film debut, I was unaware of any irony about anything—I simply worshipped my handsome, popular, and talented older brother and wanted more than ever to be just like him.

Every Friday night I would walk with Kiko to the local Macy's mall, where we would hook up with his many friends and would-be girlfriends and all go ice-skating. Kiko and I were both growing like weeds at that time, and Mom used to extend the hems of our bell-bottom jeans by periodically sewing on a band of new material—which meant that the flare of our pants got wider and wider and (because she would use corduroy or denim or whatever cloth was available) more and more colorful. I was not much of an ice-skater, and I shudder to think of the sight I must have presented flying around the rink in my gaudy elephant pants. I liked to get myself going incredibly fast—especially when the Led Zeppelin song "Rock and Roll" came on—but the only method I had mastered for stopping was to crash full speed into the wall.

My parents enrolled me for the second half of my sixth-grade year at the neighborhood middle school, and I did my best to make friends there and hang out the way I imagined my fabulous brother would have—but I just was not a natural at normal teenage social games. I remember there was a fat girl about my age who lived on the second floor of our apartment building, and I knew she was famous for having hot-and-heavy make-out sessions with many of the guys in my class—so one day when I ran into her outside our building I worked up my nerve and decided to see if I could get something going for myself. I offered her a ride on my bike, and when she accepted we went tooling around together on a short tour of the neighborhood. When the ride was over, just after she had dismounted from my Schwinn with a heavy thump, this girl turned to me and in a very businesslike manner planted her lips on mine—and then shoved her fat tongue right into my mouth. I was both amazed and thrilled, not so much by any physical or emotional stirrings the kiss produced inside me, but by the sheer unpredictability of life. Give a girl a ride on your bike—and get tongued. Who could have guessed this was how it worked? I felt I was making progress.

Mercifully, by the end of sixth grade my growing pains had disappeared and I was able to reapply my energies to a front where I was more likely to have some success: my ballet training. To return to SAB would have required scheduling another audition in New York, and I knew we didn't have the money for plane tickets. Also, we were semisettled in California by then, and Kiko was busy auditioning for acting roles there. Returning to SAB seemed impossible, so I didn't really let myself think about it. Instead my parents researched the local options, and I began taking classes at the Westside

School of Ballet in Santa Monica, an institution run by former NYCB ballerina Yvonne Mounsey and former Royal Ballet of England ballerina Rosemary Valaire. This kicked off another intense commuting schedule, back and forth on the seemingly endless journey through L.A.'s horrendous traffic, once again with my long-suffering father as my chauffeur. At Westside I made friends with a fellow dancer named Lisa Goldin, a cute little girl who lived in a huge house in Beverly Hills with a Jacuzzi in the backyard. Lisa became my first and last faux girlfriend. I remember sitting in her Jacuzzi, giggling and singing along with Patti Smith's "Because the Night," and attempting some pretty unsuccessful little kissing sessions—I had no idea what I was doing, but I kept trying, waiting for something to happen.

After several months of classes at Westside in Santa Monica, Lisa and I both started taking classes at the Los Angeles Dance Center, the affiliate school of the Los Angeles Ballet, with the famous Russian ballet teacher Irina Kosmovska. One of my classmates at my new school (where Mme Kosmovska put us through the longest combinations I believe I have ever suffered in my life) was a startlingly beautiful and talented ballerina named Darci Kistler, who was one year older than me; another was a big-jumping, dark-haired firecracker named Teresa Reyes. By the fall of my seventh-grade year, Darci had been offered a full scholarship to attend Balanchine's School of America Ballet—my old, if fleeting, alma mater—and moved to New York. I didn't talk about this much with anyone, but I still hoped I would one day return to New York and to my former school, and watching Darci head off on her adventure helped me focus on this as a goal.

When the NYCB dancer Susan Hendl, whom Mr. B sent out to scout for talent, came through Los Angeles that winter, I auditioned for the SAB summer program. To my delight I was accepted and offered a full scholarship.

This time when I headed east, my parents—perhaps assuming, or maybe hoping, I would be back at the end of the summer—stayed home. As it happened, Lisa Goldin and Teresa Reyes and I had all been accepted for that summer session in 1979, and Lisa and her mother were kind enough to invite me to share an apartment on West Sixty-sixth Street that they had sublet from a NYCB dancer who was in Saratoga Springs for the summer. (Lisa and I by this time had settled into an awkward relationship in which I tried to be a good pretend boyfriend by being a good girlfriend instead.) I was excited to be back in New York and back at the SAB, and as I began to apply myself more seriously in classes, my attitude toward ballet matured from one of happy industry to one of passion and obsession. I threw myself into my dancing as I never had before. It was an exciting time as I explored a twin love—for ballet and for New York. When the summer session was almost over I was told to report to Natasha Gleboff's office, and when she told me the school was once again offering me a full scholarship as a full-time student for the upcoming winter course, I was thrilled. I had made it back to New York and back to SAB, and this time I was going to make sure that I stayed.

Ballet-School Banquet in a Bag

LITTLE DID I know, on that day long ago when I was first invited to become a full-time student at SAB, just how long I would be staying. And little did I suspect that some thirty years later I myself would be auditioning young dancers and offering them scholarships to the school. Teaching is always a learning experience for me, and not too long after my mother passed away I had an exciting new challenge when Peter Martins decided to include a little piece I had choreographed for my intermediate-level boys' class in the SAB's annual end-of-year Workshop Performances. The kids worked like demons, and I was amazed at how good they were. Afterward I decided to thank them with a surprise graduation dinner. In the last week of school I posted a sign declaring a mandatory meeting in the teachers' lounge on Friday.

The night before the surprise feast, I cooked four dishes in bulk—Thai beef with cellophane noodles, couscous salad, tomato-and-mozzarella salad, and Mom's famous Paradise Valley potato salad. I packaged the food in gallon-size freezer bags, and made a megaload of brownies and bagged them too. The next morning I packed all of the freezer bags along with platters and serving utensils into a large rolling suitcase and took my banquet-in-a-bag with me on the subway to work. When the students showed up for the alleged meeting I surprised them with their feast. They were a little shy at first, but they quickly found their dancers' appetites, and the meal was a roaring success.

Paradise Valley Potato Salad

———

SERVES 8

This recipe for Mom's potato salad serves about eight, but it is easy to triple or quadruple the ingredients for a crowd. It is rich and creamy—and always a hit. Making it ahead of time and refrigerating it for a few hours— or even overnight—makes it even better. I have experimented with adding curry, cumin, ketchup, paprika, and even jalapeños. You can use sour cream instead of mayonnaise and Dijon mustard instead of classic yellow mustard. In fact, anything is possible—I sometimes serve this in the middle of winter with hot dogs!

8 large red potatoes
8 large eggs
1 medium red onion,
  chopped
4 stalks of celery,
  chopped
1 orange bell pepper,
  chopped

6 spears of dill pickles,
  diced
1½ cups mayonnaise
5 squirts (or about
  4 tablespoons) yellow
  mustard
3 tablespoons pickle juice
Salt and pepper

Wash your potatoes and cut them in fours, placing them in a stockpot of cold water as you work. Bring the water to a boil over high heat, and then reduce the heat to gently boil the potatoes until they are just tender—about 20 minutes. You should test them with a fork, not a knife, because as Mom would say, "You should never stab your food."

While your potatoes are cooking, place the eggs in a large pot of cold water, bring to boil, and then cover and turn the heat off. After 10 minutes (best to set a timer or you will forget) drain the eggs, rinse them under cold water, and set aside.

Place the onion, celery, bell pepper, and pickles in a large bowl and mix in your mayonnaise, mustard, and pickle juice. Peel and cut your eggs—I cut them in fours because I like them chunky—and add them to the bowl. When your potatoes are drained and cooled, add them and stir the whole mixture gently. Add salt and pepper to taste.

Cover and refrigerate for a couple of hours, so that all the flavors marry, and add salt and pepper again to taste before serving.

CHAPTER SEVEN

The Accidental Adult

I was a veteran before I was a teenager.
—MICHAEL JACKSON

In the first year after Mom died, I often had to call my father to apologize for fighting, even though I didn't realize we had been fighting until Kiko called to enlighten me. This was the way things were, on and off, for months. Pop was so rattled and lost. One alleged argument started when we were talking on the phone, and out of the blue, Pop burst into tears and shouted, "Why do you dislike me so much? Why have you always hated me?" And then he hung up.

All I had done to provoke this was to tell Pop that I loved him and that I would send him some more money for his bills. Luis and I had been trying to pick up more and more of his expenses, paying his credit cards and other monthly debts. It was sad, because I could track his lonely wanderings around the country by the credit-card charges—a six-dollar dinner at Souper Salad in Santa Fe, a four-dollar meal at McDonald's in Gallup, New Mexico, a tank of gas in Chinle, Arizona. This last charge, in fact, was how I discovered at one point that Pop had driven back to the reservation to visit Mom's sisters and have a session with my uncle Joe, our medicine man. Evidently they all asked him to come live with them, and let them take care of him—which strikes me as highly ironic given that for so many years everyone in Mom's family disapproved so strongly of my non-Navajo father. The idea of my father living on the reservation was preposterous—there is nothing there but a gas station, a Burger King and a McDonald's (can't have one without the other), and a grocery store called Bashas. You can get two channels on the TV. Sure enough, when Pop went there, he didn't last a week. He told me it was too hot, there was nothing to do, and there was nothing on the television, so he got bored and he left. That's my dad.

As I explored my "living past" it made me feel guilty to realize how strained and painful my relationship with my father had been for so much of my life. Maybe Pop had been revisiting our problematic relationship too—maybe that's what caused his strange outburst over the phone. I know some fighting is inevitable between fathers and sons, and in my case, my emerging homosexuality during adolescence definitely complicated the relationship with my macho pop. And of course, my resentment of my father's infidelities as a husband did not help our relationship. As I look back, I can see that at no time were things tenser between us than in the months when I was first launching my new life as a full-time student at the SAB in New York.

When I called my parents on that summer evening in 1979 with my exciting news, I'm sure I never, for one instant, paused to think about the havoc I might be causing for the rest of my family. I guess I was already floating through life in that bubble of selfishness that the teenage ego spins for itself, a self-contained and self-reflecting world in which *my* needs and *my* desires and *my* hopes and *my* fears were all that existed. It was the end of July when I made that call home, and by the end of August Mom and Pop and Kiko had all picked up and moved to New York. Kiko had been offered a role in a PBS television pilot that was being filmed in Boston, and I tried to convince myself that the East Coast seemed like the best option for all of us at the time. But increasingly, as I look back, I am struck by the sacrifices everyone in my family seems to have made for me when I was very young—and I feel some late-blooming guilt.

My parents and Kiko and I settled into a small apartment in the Rego Park section of Queens, and poor Kiko was enrolled in some local high school (in a recent phone conversation he reminded me that he attended four different high schools over four years). My father and I began what would turn out to be our last session of daily commutes together— and our ugliest, both in terms of traffic and clashing personalities—driving back and forth from the apartment in Rego Park to my ballet classes at the Juilliard School in Manhattan.

Fourteen is a notoriously unattractive age for all boys; still, I shudder when I think about the way I treated my parents during those months while we were living together in New York. I was attending ballet classes during the day, and hanging around Lincoln Center between classes and in the evenings as much as I could, sneaking into performances, soaking up anything and everything that I could about ballet. Many of my fellow students were enrolled in the Professional

Children's School, which allowed them to squeeze their aca-
demic studies in between the intense demands of classes at
SAB, but we couldn't afford the $3,000 tuition (it's an as-
tronomical $35,000 today). Instead, my parents enrolled me
in correspondence courses for the eighth grade. I was completely uninterested in these courses, and I remember sitting at dinner one night and announcing to my mother and
father that schoolwork was a waste of time and that I wasn't
going to bother with it anymore. They looked at each other
and then at me, and began to try to argue that this really
wasn't a choice, that I had to keep up with my studies—but
we all knew that I had taken the bit in my teeth and would
do as I pleased.

Another source of irritation between my parents and me
in those days was the monthly stipend of $250 for living ex-
penses that SAB gave me. The expectation was that I would
turn this money over to my father as soon as I got it, and in
retrospect I can see that this was completely reasonable—my
entire family had moved to New York to allow me to pursue
my ballet career. My parents were both working to support
all of us here. But at the time the adolescent monster in me re-
sented having to hand over what I considered to be *my* money.
After a couple of months of seething at the unfairness of all
this, I decided to try an experiment. When I received my next
check for $250, I didn't mention it to my parents but went to
the bank and cashed the check myself. Giddy with my green-
backs, I went directly from the bank on a big spending spree,
splurging on about forty dollars' worth of candy. When I got
home I stashed my candy (a mother lode of M&M's Peanuts
and Reese's Pieces, as I recall) and my leftover cash in my

underwear drawer. I felt triumphant—I was a cunning and clever Candy Lord. When my father asked me repeatedly during the next week if I had received my check yet, I just shrugged my shoulders and shook my head.

Kiko and I were both getting to be pretty big boys by this time, and when either of us ran short of socks or underwear, we would, with the selfish self-sufficiency of teenagers, walk across the hall and raid our father's dresser. It had never once occurred to me that when my father ran out of socks or underwear he might reverse the raid—but he did, and this was how I got caught in my lies about the check. Pop was furious when he found all that money stuffed away under my candy one morning, and the scene where he took back the money and confronted me was not pretty.

On the drive to ballet school later that same morning, Pop and I didn't speak. The car was a rolling rage cage. That night NYCB had a special gala to raise money for the school, and several kids, including me, had volunteered to sell raffle tickets before the show. As I got out of the car, I told Pop that he should come a half hour later than usual that evening, that I would be inside the New York State Theater doing the raffle thing, but then I would come find him and we would go home.

Principal dancers Sean Lavery and Heather Watts were performing that night in Peter Martins's *Rossini Pas de Deux*. I was dying to watch my idols work their magic, and after the raffle sale was over, although I knew I should go find my father and head home, I allowed myself just one peek inside the theater. Of course I ended up staying for the entire program—there was no way I could leave.

When the performance was finally over I ambled out into the dark Manhattan night, dizzy with excitement and emotion from what I had just seen—and there was my father, waiting for me in the white van he had leased when he and Mom moved to New York. When I got into the car there was dead silence, and we drove over the Queensboro Bridge and all the way home without saying a word. It was not until we were back in the apartment that he followed me into my bedroom and spun me around to face him and began shouting at me: "Why did you make me wait for three and a half hours? What were you doing in there?" I looked at him and shrugged. "I wanted to see the performance," I answered, as if this should have been perfectly obvious to anyone. And then we both exploded. He shoved me onto my bed and started yelling at me and I began to scream hysterically, "That was *my* money, that was *my* money! And I wanted to see the ballet!"

The incident marked a turning point for Pop and me. We stopped speaking to each other and coexisted with a wall of resentment between us. When he drove me to ballet school, I would just stare out the window, dying for the moment when I could get out of the car and away from him. I'm sure the commute was equally unpleasant for him. It was a miserable situation—so miserable that not much later I came up with what I thought was a brilliant solution for all of us. Mom and Pop and Kiko and I were all standing on the little balcony overlooking the street at our Queens apartment when I decided to share my idea.

"Guess what! I've decided to move out!" I announced with a happy smile. There was dead silence, followed immediately by a horrendous crashing explosion from somewhere below us on the street. My parents looked at each other and then we all looked over the railing to see what had happened. A car that had come racing around the corner had just smashed into my father's white van.

"That's it!" my father screamed. "I hate it here! We're getting the fuck out!"

Pop meant what he said, and he did what he meant. Within days he and Mom and Kiko had packed up and moved out of our apartment in Queens. I know that leaving me alone in New York must have been difficult for my mother—she said as much many times in later years. But she too had tired of the hardships of the city, and her instincts as a dutiful wife told her she should stick with my father. I remember Mom and Pop and Kiko all drove me to my ballet classes on the morning of the day they were leaving. I stood outside the Juilliard School and waved good-bye. I was fourteen, and totally on my own in New York City. I had $250 a month to live on and no place to live yet, but I had launched my ballet dream. I was in heaven.

My introduction to the glamorous life in the big city began not long after my parents' departure with a classic New York experience: eviction. My fellow SAB student Jefferson Baum and I considered ourselves complete geniuses when we landed a cheap place to live in the upper nineties—but only a few days after moving in we found ourselves back on the street. Evidently we had a sublet of a sublet. Discouraged and with nowhere to go, we threw ourselves at the mercy of two fellow dancers, Einar Thordarson and Afshin Mofid, who had rented an apartment on the top floor of a Sixty-ninth Street brownstone. We begged them to let us squat with them for just a few days while we figured things out, and as we were all in that "the more the merrier" stage of life, of course they said yes. Somehow a few days bled into a few more days, and a short visit became a technically illegal overoccupancy. I remember one day all four of us boys were practicing our double air tours over and over in the apartment, when suddenly there was a knock on our door. When we opened it, there stood the owner and landlord—Edward Villella. The man whose gravity-defying leaps had first impassioned me for ballet when I was only four years old was their landlord, and he lived downstairs. Apparently his chandelier had been swinging back and forth so wildly as a result of our double air tours he was afraid it was going to fall. He asked us to please stop—and then he took a second, more studied look at Jefferson and me. We were busted.

Afshin and Einar immediately jumped to our defense, explaining that we had nowhere else to live, and begged him to let us stay. After a long silence, Mr. Villella gave us another long look—and nodded. Jefferson and I could stay, provided we each paid $175 a month in extra rent. We didn't have a dedicated bedroom—Jefferson and I just set up our beds in the living room—but we had a home. We were thrilled.

My tenure in Mr. Villella's house was the beginning of a long and happy period for me. My roommates and I danced and trained together at SAB all day every day, and generally took care of one another in our life outside the school. After paying my rent I had only $75 left every month to buy groceries and eat, but my teenage roommates seemed to be in more or less the same spot, and we all worked together to keep one another going. I was probably the most experienced cook in the group—Kiko and I had run a fried-dough concession as boys, after all, and we had often cooked ourselves simple meals when we were home alone after school, waiting for our parents to get back from work. Whenever my SAB roommates and I went grocery shopping we would buy things like Hamburger Helper and ground meat, canned vegetables, pasta, and bottled Ragu sauce. Tuna casserole with Ruffles crumbled on top was a particular house favorite. Humble as these dishes may sound, a few simple tricks made them pretty delicious, and because they were easy to make in bulk no one had to hold back on seconds and thirds.

Our apartment had a little terrace with a hibachi grill, and in good weather we would barbecue a megaload of hot dogs and invite some friends over to dine alfresco. I will never forget the chilly December night when John Lennon was shot outside his home at the Dakota, just a few blocks away. We joined the rest of the neighborhood in an all-night vigil in his honor. After making an enormous vat of mac 'n' cheese to feed any visiting mourners, we placed our speakers in our front windows overlooking the street and blasted Lennon's beautiful song "Imagine" into the cold night air.

When I think back to this period I am surprised by how seamlessly I dropped out of any semblance of a family life into a completely unchaperoned life with a pack of boys. I remember no loneliness, no fear. I was a dance addict, and I was so thrilled to be in Balanchine's school and living in New York that nothing else mattered. I was in the advanced men's class at the school and one of our teachers, Stanley Williams, was so renowned that many of the big ballet stars in the company— male and female—would come and take class with us. I would

stare in awe whenever dancers like Peter Martins, Robert
Weiss, Helgi Tomasson, Ib Andersen, and Joseph Duell joined
us—I found it difficult to concentrate. And of course I nearly
fainted the first time Rudolf Nureyev walked in—sometimes
he would come straight from the airport, having flown over
on a Concord specifically to take Stanley's class. The dressing
room would always empty in a hurry whenever Rudy arrived,
for he had quite a foul mouth and a creative and seemingly
endless supply of lewd comments. He never changed himself
but had an attendant who put his dance clothes on for him.
I watched this exotic behavior with wide eyes, knowing that
the moment Rudy stepped into the studio nothing in the world
would matter except his dancing.

All of my teachers at the school—Stanley Williams, Andrei Kramarevsky, and Richard Rapp—were completely dedicated to the job of instilling the art of classical ballet into our
young bodies, but in the process they were also instilling important behavioral lessons about respect and hard work and
deportment in general. Classes required 100 percent of one's
attention and 100 percent of one's effort 100 percent of the
time—period. To fidget or yawn was a misdemeanor, punish-
able by expulsion from class. Stanley Williams was particularly fascinating to me. He was very gentle and quiet—in fact,
he rarely spoke—but very clear and precise in his actions. I
would watch him carefully in class every day, trying to mimic
his movements as precisely as possible, and I could actually
feel myself learning to dance. It was thrilling.

Of course whenever Balanchine came to watch class a
buzz ran through the whole school. He would always stop by
the office first to check in with Natasha Gleboff, so the word

would get out that he was in the vicinity. Then he would do a walk-in, appearing in the classroom unannounced, and stand there, watching our combinations. He was always impeccably dressed in a well-fitted jacket and knit pants and beautiful shoes, a scarf at his neck and his hair slicked back—to me he looked like a movie star. Stanley would always go over and say hello to Mr. B, while the rest of us just held our breath and stood still as statues. On a few occasions Lincoln Kirstein came in with Balanchine, and then the excitement level was over the top. These two men represented what all of us were living for—they were walking icons, the original founders of the meaning of life as we knew it.

The talent among the students at SAB was always very impressive to me, and in the spring of my first year there was great excitement when my former California classmate Darci Kistler attained the Holy Grail—Balanchine asked her to join the New York City Ballet. Typically only about 10 percent of the students attending SAB were invited to join Balanchine's company, and to be picked at the young age of sixteen was also unusual. Later that year, after Darci had joined the company, I snuck into the theater to watch her perform George Balanchine's *Symphony in C*. (A fellow student who delivered the flowers at the end of the performances used to leave an exit door cracked open; I would sneak in and sit in the fifth ring and then, taking note of which seats were empty, gradually work my way down toward the front between ballets.) I had heard about Darci's performance in this ballet, and particularly about the second-movement pas de deux, but I was unprepared for what I was about to witness. When the music started and Darci started dancing, I was carried off to a dreamworld inhabited by a stunning angel in white. The whole theater gasped with me, and when the pas de deux was over—despite the NYCB de-emphasis on "stars" and over-drawn applause—the audience exploded. They would not let Darci leave the stage, but called her back again and again with endless rounds of applause. It was entirely inadvertent on Darci's part, but she had simply stopped the ballet. It was an amazing moment, and I couldn't believe my good fortune to be there to witness it. I couldn't have imagined then that I would one day partner her in that same movement.

Little by little I was having some tiny triumphs of my own that first year, and when the time came for the SAB Workshop Performances at the end of the year, I landed some nice roles. Stanley Williams chose my schoolmate Dagoberto Nieves and me to perform August Bournonville's *Jockey Dance* and two Bournonville solos from *Napoli*; Joseph Duell, a princi-pal dancer who was debuting as a choreographer, cast me and my fellow student Joseph Malbrough as the leads in his new ballet *Jubilee*. We would rehearse after our normal school day, usually from seven to nine at night, and I remember de-veloping an enormous crush on Duell in these sessions.

It seems so obvious to me now why I might have become infatuated with Duell, or why I sometimes found it hard to concentrate when the male ballet stars decided to join us in class. (I find it hard to believe, but sometime after my retire-ment Peter Martins told me that those big stars I was star-ing at in Stanley's class were also staring back at me, flabber-gasted that a fifteen-year-old boy was executing dance moves they had been working years to master. Peter tends to flatter me.) Back then, as a fifteen-year-old import from the Arizona desert, I was still puzzled by my own sexuality, and innocent about sex in general. The school and the company were both hotbeds of sexually charged adolescents and young adults, and I was well aware of all the clasping and grasping and flirting and pining and sighing and yearning in play around me. But I didn't think about my own role in this exchange too specifically. Weren't dancers supposed to be both passionate and physically expressive? And weren't we all dancers?

Then one day my roommate Jefferson asked me to go have lunch with him. We went to Vinny's Pizza on Amsterdam, where the pizza was both excellent and cheap, and as we were eating Jefferson launched into what he has since referred to as "The Talk." (As in, "Remember when I took you out for some pizza and 'The Talk,' Jock?")

"I know they've been hitting on you, Jock, and I feel like you're starting to go the other way," Jefferson said, breaking the ice about halfway through our lunch. I smiled and took a bite of pizza. "You don't have to let this happen—you have a choice, you know," Jefferson continued. I smiled and took a sip of Coke. "You don't *want* to go the other way, do you, Jock?" Jefferson asked. "I mean, if you do that's fine. That's your business. But I don't want you to get pushed into something you don't actually want. It's okay to say no to people. Do you *want* to go the other way, Jock?" I smiled again, but still said nothing.

I never gave Jefferson answers to his questions that day, but I think our discussion helped me answer the same questions for myself. Yes, I was "going the other way," as he had put it. I was attracted to men, not women. Somehow I had learned this truth—or had learned how to acknowledge it to myself in a calm and straightforward way—in this simple one-sided conversation with my trusted friend. And I had discovered something else, too. I had discovered the power and comfort and safety that can come with saying nothing. I had found a lovely little refuge in this wild New York world that I had landed in so suddenly—a refuge called silence.

I did not have a normal family home life, or a normal teenage school life in New York. But I did have two reliable platforms for stabilizing my existence: I could dance, and I could keep quiet. And I was pretty good at both.

A Little Hamburger Helper and My Friends

GROWING TEENAGE BOYS are notorious for having large appetites, but growing teenage boys who dance all day take the art of hoovering food to a new level. I witness this first-hand every day when my young students at the SAB file into the cafeteria for their lunch. Thirty years ago, when I was a student at SAB, we had no dorms and no cafeteria—which meant my roommates and I had to shop and cook for ourselves on our very meager budgets. We stuck to basics, but over time we developed our own signature touches for our communal meals—sausage with Hamburger Helper, crumbled Ruffles potato chips atop tuna casserole, or big chunks of the cheapest cheddar we could find stirred in to create cheesy land mines in our spaghetti casseroles.

Even though I am allegedly a true grown-up now instead of an accidental adult, I sometimes feel more like an accidental adolescent. After all, I am around impossibly young people all day. When I get a craving for one of the simple but satisfying meals of my youth, I put on my workout clothes and some good seventies or eighties music and make this updated version of my old standby.

The Accidental Adolescent's Grown-up Version of Hamburger Helper

SERVES 8

Salt

10 links sweet and spicy
sausage, 5 of each,
removed from casings
(about 1¾ pounds)

1 large white onion, diced

5 cloves garlic, finely diced

1 tablespoon dried oregano

1 12-ounce can diced
tomatoes

1 10¾-ounce can
condensed cream of
potato soup

Pepper

1-pound box dried pasta
(bow tie, or farfalle,
pasta is what I use)

½ to 1 cup grated
Parmesan cheese (store-
bought, grated is fine)

Put a large pot of water on to boil for the pasta, and salt it generously.

Brown your sausage in a large pot or pan, breaking it up so that it becomes ground meat. Add your onion, garlic, and oregano and cook for about 5 to 10 minutes on high heat, depending on your stove. Keep watch and stir regularly so your ingredients don't stick to the bottom of the pan. Add the tomatoes and bring the mixture a boil; then turn the heat down to medium. Cook for about 10 minutes more, and then add your cream of potato soup and cover partially. (This is when I take out a potato masher and squash the ingredients, so that everything becomes a uniform size.) Cook for another 10 minutes and add salt and pepper to taste. At this point you can reduce the heat to low and let the meat sauce simmer while you prepare your pasta.

When your water has come to rolling boil, throw the pasta in and cook for two minutes less than the directions on the box recommend, so that the pasta is very al dente. Turn off the heat. Remove the pasta from the boiling water with a slotted spoon and put it directly into the sauce.

If the mixture is looking too thick, ladle in some of the pasta water to get the desired texture. Add a handful of Parmesan cheese and stir. I like a lot of cheese and usually keep going until I am happy with the gooeyness of it all. When the dish is to your liking, take it to the table and serve with some Italian bread and extra Parmesan on the side.

CHAPTER EIGHT

First Love, First Job, First Trip, First Tiramisu

Cooking is like love. It should be entered into with abandon or not at all.
—HARRIET VAN HORNE

The first time I noticed the handsome blond man staring across the dance studio in my general direction I looked over my right shoulder to see who was behind me. No one. When I looked across the room again he was still standing there, leaning against the piano, staring—so I looked over my left shoulder to check out who the lucky person was. No one. Then my jaw dropped in disbelief. I blushed. Me?

He smiled.

I couldn't believe it. I had seen Ulrik in our advanced men's class on several occasions in the last few weeks, and I had developed a raging teenage crush from a distance. He was Danish, a former dancer with the Royal Danish Ballet whom Peter Martins had brought in to join the NYCB corps de ballet. He was nine years older than I, with intense bright blue eyes. We barely spoke to each other, but in the few words we did exchange his elegant accent seemed to imply that here was a man of intelligence, humor, sophistication, and charm. Basically, I was a goner from the start.

Mutual admiration was all that Ulrik and I shared at first. There were certain obstacles blocking anything else. For one thing, I was still fifteen and I had no idea what "being in love" entailed in practical terms. What did one actually do, besides gawk and sigh? And then there was the fact that Ulrik was involved with another man—a rather prominent man in the ballet world. For me it was thrilling enough that we could be around each other, in each other's orbit for a part of the day. In ballet classes back then, between the barre and center portions of our exercises, everybody would take out their cigarettes and smoke. Stanley Williams would light up his pipe and then everyone would get their nicotine fix. (This would never, ever happen now.) Whenever he came to take our men's class, Ulrik and I would stare at each other all through the class and all through the breaks, and my heart would always idle at a higher speed; the looks and glances, the fleeting touches and occasional passing remarks that we shared all served to stoke the fire.

It was spring and I thought I might be falling in love—and to make things perfect, I seemed to be dancing more than ever. Recently Peter Martins—who was already multitasking as one of the company's most admired principal dancers and as an up-and-coming choreographer in his own right—had been named ballet master with Balanchine, Jerome Robbins, and John Taras. One day Peter called me into a studio with my fellow SAB student Katrina Killian (who would become a particular favorite of Balanchine's before long) and began working with us. That was how I discovered that Peter had decided to choreograph a new interpretation of the ballet *The Magic Flute* on me and Katrina. (To choreograph a ballet "on" a dancer—that is, to create a work with and for a specific artist—is a peculiar idiom of the ballet world. Strange as it may sound to the lay ear, to a seasoned dancer it sounds even stranger to use any other preposition.) I was excited for all sorts of reasons, professional and personal. Peter was an object of worship among most of us students, and to work closely with him was everyone's dream. I had been cast in the role of Luke, the peasant boy who falls in love with Lise, and Katrina and I were scheduled to premiere the ballet for the school's annual Workshop Performances. Peter's girlfriend at the time was the brilliant and edgy Heather Watts, and my secret heartthrob, Ulrik, happened to be Peter's fellow countryman and close friend—so increased proximity to both Heather and Ulrik would be an accidental advantage.

For that same year's Workshop Performances, in addition to my role in *Magic Flute*, Suki Schorer had cast me as the male lead for a performance of Balanchine's *La Source*, and Joseph Duell had chosen me for a pas de trois in his new ballet *La Création du Monde*. Peter's *Magic Flute* was a full-blown "story" ballet with very intricate and fast partnering and its own elaborate set, while Duell's piece was a more modern, jazzy number, with a very retro costume—I remember wearing a unitard with something that resembled macramé strings dangling from the ankles and wrists. The challenges of these dramatically different ballets and the high level of talent and sophistication of the people I was working with were all a little intimidating to me at the time—in so many ways I was still just a young boy from the desert. It makes me laugh to remember how I used to try to field Ulrik's flirtations when he was in my class and then, in my free time between classes, head over to the Metropolitan Opera House where I would amuse myself by sliding down the railing of the long escalator to the parking lot over and over again, like a ten-year-old kid, until the guard got pissed off and told me to stop.

The Workshop Performances got a lot of press that May, and Anna Kisselgoff of the *New York Times* singled me out as "a highly talented dancer of magnificent stage presence." Although the praise gave me a nice warm feeling for a few minutes, I knew that kudos of this sort didn't mean much in the long run. In ballet you had to prove yourself moment by moment, and every day offered a thousand different opportunities to fail. I was painfully aware of what a primitive I was, compared to almost everyone around me, and I was particularly self-conscious about not having the classic ballet dancer's tall, lean build. I was young and green, but I was also incredibly determined. My hope was that if I listened and watched carefully, kept quiet, threw my heart into everything I did, and kept pushing myself with new challenges, I could get better.

One of my most exciting challenges came later that June when Balanchine staged a special Tchaikovsky Festival in honor of the Russian composer, with ten days of performances featuring his music in repertory ballets as well as in twelve new works by Balanchine, Duell, Jacques d'Amboise, Peter Martins, Jerome Robbins, and John Taras. As part of a new program of selections from ballets, called Tempo di Valse, Taras was choreographing the waltz from *Eugene Onegin* on me and seven other students at the school—and we were going to premiere it at the festival. I had just turned sixteen that April, and now—for ten days, anyway—I would be dancing with the NYCB itself, representing the school in real performances for huge audiences.

The stage setting for the Tchaikovsky Festival was designed by Philip Johnson and John Burgee and consisted of translucent tubing that was hung and lit in different architectural configurations—in my opinion the tubing was ugly, and it smelled bad to boot. But the festival itself was thrilling, nonetheless. Balanchine had decided that we students dancing *Eugene Onegin* would close the Tempo di Valse program, which was a way to honor and highlight the school. The ballet that came right before our piece was the "Waltz of the Flowers," danced by Heather Watts with the corps, and my fellow students and I would stand in the wings in our little outfits, watching, and thinking, "Oh my God. We have to follow this?" Heather brought the house down every night. I mean, literally. She had to bow at least five times. I watched with awe, fascinated by her angular body and her long legs and beautiful feet, and by the exciting combination of precision and abandon she brought to her role. I was smitten—as far as I was concerned, she was a goddess. Anna Kisselgoff must have agreed, because she christened Heather "The Queen of the Festival."

Dancing in the Tchaikovsky Festival that June was a thrill for me professionally, and it was also the kickoff for considerable excitement in my private life. The barely suppressed romance between Ulrik and me had been getting hotter and hotter, and when the two of us were thrown into backstage evenings together during the Tchaikovsky Festival, the situation reached the boiling point. Ulrik was living in an apartment in SoHo with Julia Gruen, a friend and former SAB student, and one night when he and I were both at a party after the evening's performances he invited me home with him. I accepted, of course. I blush to think of how naive I was at that stage in my life. I literally had no idea about the mechanics of sex (I think again of my mother when she met my father), but like any good horny teenager, I guess I must have caught on quickly enough. My teenage infatuation with Ulrik was soon a full-blown love affair.

I was already pretty dizzy with all the new developments in my life when, shortly after the Tchaikovsky Festival, I was summoned, along with three other dancers—Espen Giljane, Sabrina Pillars, and Lisa Jackson—to take a company class with George Balanchine. None of us had any idea why we had been called in, but I remember how excited I was just to be in the big rehearsal studio on the fifth floor of the New York State Theater at Lincoln Center (now renamed the David H. Koch Theater), where so many famous dancers had worked—the same studio where Jerome Robbins and Mr. B himself had choreographed on their dancers. I was standing at the barre, young and eager, feeling closer than ever to realizing the dream I had carried around inside me since I was four. Balanchine was watching me as I did my pliés, the most basic combination, and as he watched he shook his head and said, "No." I did my pliés again, and again he said, "No." I tried a third time, and once again he said, "No." And then he walked away. I was devastated—the truth had been exposed!

Obviously I was devoid of all talent. When class was over, ballet mistress Rosemary Dunleavy walked all four of us visiting students down the hall to the elevator in silence. Just as the elevator doors were about to close on us, she congratulated us and announced that Balanchine had invited all four of us to join the NYCB corps de ballet.

That moment when Mr. B invited me to become a dancer with the New York City Ballet will always remain one of the high points of my life. There were no cell phones in those days, so that evening I went to a pay phone in the street to call my parents and give them the news. They sounded excited for me, happy my career seemed to be really taking off, but also preoccupied by things that were going on in their world out west. I remember having a hollow feeling after I hung up the phone. Our conversation had made it so clear to me how different and disconnected our lives had become—there was so much going on in my life that my family didn't know about and that I wasn't about to tell them. I could only assume the reverse must also be true. I walked home to my room on the top floor of Edward Villella's town house in a strange, bittersweet state of mind, feeling incredibly happy and incredibly sad at the same time.

As it turned out, my colleagues and I would be the last four dancers chosen by Balanchine before he died. Even without knowing this, I felt deeply honored by his invitation, and I was determined to prove myself worthy. I worked harder than ever in my own classes and rehearsals, and watched every rehearsal and performance I could, paying particular attention to the way the star couples—Heather Watts and Bart Cook, Darci Kistler and Sean Lavery, Peter Martins and Suzanne

Farrell, Patricia McBride and Helgi Tomasson—partnered each other. The smoothness, the complexity of movement, the way the lines between their two bodies blended and through a series of physical actions evoked a magical beauty—that was what I wanted to create someday. I tried to carry my observations back with me to my own work, and gradually I began to feel that I might be at the threshold of understanding ballet on a deeper, more intuitive level. Progress required hours and hours of work, but there were definitely some breakthrough moments for me, both as a dancer and as an observer. I will never forget the performance, for instance, when I "saw" Suzanne Farrell for the first time, in the sense of truly understanding her extraordinary talent. She was dancing the "Diamonds" pas de deux from *Jewels* with Peter Martins, and I was standing in the wings, watching. Suzanne was so beautiful and otherworldly I could barely breathe. I wanted to nudge the people around me and ask them if they could believe what they were seeing. Afterward I was still standing in the wings, watching, as all the corps and soloists filed away, leaving Balanchine alone with principal dancers Suzanne and Peter Martins. I often tried to eavesdrop on these little sessions when Balanchine would huddle with the stars of the evening to go over their performance, hoping to learn from his comments. He was leaning in toward Suzanne, looking at her intensely, talking to her. I couldn't hear what he was saying, but a moment later, as he turned and wandered off as if in a dream, it seemed to me that, although Balanchine had created this ballet and seen it many times before, he had been as moved and dazzled by this performance as any member of the audience on that night.

I threw my entire being into what was now my official "profession"—and I immersed myself just as passionately in my love affair with my older boyfriend. Our relationship was not something that I took lightly. I was sixteen, and head-over-heels in love for the first time in the way that only teenagers can be in love. Everything in life felt so charged and exciting, and to the little "Puerto Rican–Indian ballet sissy" from Arizona that still lurked inside me, the world seemed to be expanding at an amazing rate, getting bigger and brighter on every front with every day. That July I traveled with the company to the annual summer season in Saratoga Springs for the first time, and my friend Espen and I, along with Ulrik and another wonderful dancer in the corps named John Bass, stayed together in a house on Saratoga Lake. I rehearsed my heart out all day, and in the downtime between and after rehearsals and performances I hung around the edges of the brilliant and witty older crowd that Ulrik was part of, watching and listening and trying to master their social jargon. On Sundays I was dumbfounded when Ulrik and John Bass whipped through the *New York Times* crossword puzzle in less than an hour—I couldn't even get a quarter of the way through Monday's puzzle, which was the easiest. I was self-conscious about my lack of formal education—the last formal classroom I had been in was my seventh-grade year in California. I listened carefully to the animated conversations all around me, trying to decipher the multilingual puns and one-liners that for the most part flew right over my head. I knew this was not a world I could compete in, so I didn't try.

At first Ulrik and I tried to keep our relationship secret, not only because he was supposedly still involved with another man but also because of my tender age. I don't think we did a very good job of being discreet, because at a certain point word came down from higher-ups at SAB that Ulrik should break it off with me—or else. I believe there was a suggestion that my parents might have to be contacted if we didn't stop seeing each other. This was a devastating turn of events for me, and when Ulrik bowed to the authorities and broke up with me—by telephone—I started bawling like a two-year-old. I felt it was the end of my world, and I was inconsolable.

I returned to Edward Villella's town house after the summer session in Saratoga in a tumultuous state of mind, and when I discovered that the boy who had sublet from me had left everything in tatters—trash everywhere and my bed a gritty horror—I had a kind of meltdown. Sobbing and swearing, fueled by the raging hormones of a brokenhearted teenage boy, I packed all of my belongings in a huge old rusty metal trunk that was my only luggage, called my fellow dancer and new friend Lisa Jackson to ask if I could come stay with her for a while, and moved out.

My intention had been to nurse my broken heart in anonymous and unknown surroundings, but as it turned out, my love crisis—like so many teenage love tragedies—was short-lived. Ulrik and I soon decided to ignore the authorities and get back together. August is often a nonworking (and unpaid) month for the NYCB, and Ulrik, Julia, John Bass, and Julia's parents had all made plans to head to the island of Hydra in Greece, where they had rented a house. When Ulrik suggested that I join him there later that month, I was thrilled. My first trip to Europe, on a mission to be with my beloved.

I don't believe I consulted anyone about this trip. When

I received the first tax refund of my life, for $980, I simply cashed it and bought myself a round-trip ticket to Athens—which left me $20 to live on for the rest of the month. I cringe when I remember my arrival in Athens on that first European trip of my life. I had dressed for my travels in cowboy boots and khaki pants and a bright orange shirt with gold stripes and a leather vest, and I was lugging THE TRUNK—the rusted metal monstrosity, crammed with my life's possessions. Ulrik had come over from the island to meet me at the Athens airport, and he took one look at me and collapsed into laughter. "Is this your *suitcase?*" he asked. He looked tanned and breezy in his perfect-for-the-Mediterranean khaki shorts and sandals.

That whole trip was so exotic and surreal for me—I felt as if my already incredible expanding universe got supersized in those two weeks. We traveled to Hydra by hydrofoil, and when we reached the island Ulrik explained to me that there were no cars there. "We will need a donkey," he said, eyeing my trunk. But all the donkeys and all the donkey boys were taking their afternoon siesta—so Ulrik and I each grabbed one end of the trunk, and in the blazing midafternoon heat we wrestled that bastard up the steep stone steps that cross-hatch Hydra's seaside cliffs, all the way to the next little fishing village, where our house was perched high above the blue Aegean.

The magic of my first visit to that Greek island is something that will never leave me. The physical drama of the land itself and the way the light raked across it, the sounds of the donkeys and roosters and dogs, the way the smell of the salty sea mixed with that of the pungent dry hills—all of these thrilled me. I had experienced the desert of Arizona, the streets of New York, and the suburbs of Los Angeles, but Hydra gave me my first real taste of the varieties of experience the planet can offer. The trip expanded my understanding of beauty, and my appetite for new places and experiences. The people we met, an eclectic mix of artists and wanderers from all parts of the world, seemed equally exotic. We made friends with the painter Brice Marden and his wife, Helene, who had a house on the island, and with an eccentric beach-comber named Von Furstenburg. At night we partied until the sun came up, and on our 6 a.m. walks home we dove off the ancient seawalls into the salty sea. When Heather Watts arrived by hydrofoil one afternoon, the glamour quotient of our little group—and the testosterone levels of all the het-erosexual men on the island—bumped up several notches. Everything felt dreamlike and magical—as if I had landed in a Mediterranean version of the *Nutcracker* with my very own Prince. When Julia and I had to head back to New York before the others, I stepped onto the hydrofoil that would take me to Athens and took one last look at Ulrik—tanned and wearing only his shorts, smoking a cigarette, and waving good-bye from the dock—and fell sobbing into Julia's arms.

By the late fall of my first season with the NYCB, Ulrik and I had moved into a two-bedroom floor-through in Chel-sea with Julia, who, over the course of the summer, had become my dear friend as well (and remains so to this day). As a new company member, I was dancing nonstop, I was madly in love, and I even seemed to be establishing a kind of surrogate family in New York through my various connec-tions within the dance world. There was a comforting sense of domesticity to my evenings at home with Ulrik and Julia, when we all cooked and ate together. Julia often invited us to join her at her parents' house for dinners and other exotic soirees, affording me glimpses into a world and a way of life I never knew existed. The Gruens lived (and still live) in a vast apartment that is filled with books and antiques and is redolent of that shabby-chic aura that seems to settle around lives of unpretentious intelligence and elegance. Evenings at the Gruens' were always exciting in the purest sense because you never knew who would show up or where the evening would go. On many occasions we would all dress up in black tie, just for the hell of it, and the evening would take on the festive feel of a bygone era. After dinner there would often be piano playing and singing, and always plenty of "chaaam-pers" and art-world anecdotes courtesy of Julia's writer-photographer father, John. The Gruens will always have a special place in my heart, and I sometimes wish I could go back and sit at the Gruens' dinner table once more and discover what on earth I was thinking. The world I had landed in was a far cry from the house in Paradise Valley, Arizona, that I had left behind.

The company and conversation at these soirees dazzled me, but I was not about to jump into the fray myself—the chance that I would say something astoundingly stupid was just too great. Often I would retire to the kitchen to watch Julia's mother, the accomplished artist Jane Wilson, prepare our elaborate meals, helping her whenever I could. Watching Jane work in the kitchen or set a table taught me so much about entertaining with elegance and style. Those sessions were also when I first discovered how much I loved to cook. Jane was a wonderful and inventive chef, and the beautiful roasts and elegant desserts she turned out seemed nothing less than a miracle to me. I began experimenting more and more with cooking at home—with erratic results. I remember the first meal I made for Ulrik, Julia, and John Bass—a dense, rock-hard, way-overcooked meat loaf that slipped off the serving platter when I tripped on the rug and then went bouncing like a small bowling ball across the floor. Everybody politely stifled their laughter, and we all choked down the runaway entrée after I maneuvered it back onto its platter. I had another disaster on New Year's Eve, when I decided to make my first Caesar salad. In my eagerness to have everything ready on time, I made the salad and dressed it that afternoon—and it sat until midnight, at which point it was a soggy, inedible pile of green mush.

Probably my most painful cooking episode was one that also taught me an important lesson about culinary hubris. In a fit of confidence I decided to contribute to the bounty at the Gruen household by bringing a homemade tiramisu to one of our gatherings. I didn't know what mascarpone was at the time, and when there was none at the grocery store I substituted another exotic-sounding cheese—Gorgonzola—figuring it would do just fine. I transported my masterpiece in a pan with foil over it, and I should have realized from the sloshing and spillage in the taxi on the way over that something was wrong. The smell alone was unbearable, and as I climbed the stairs to the Gruens' apartment I began to panic. What had I been thinking? Maybe nobody would notice—or, better yet, maybe nobody had ever had tiramisu.

Wait a minute—hadn't John Gruen lived in Italy? I was humiliated as I presented my sloppy, swampy-smelling creation, and angry with myself for daring to impose such a pathetic failure on others. I made a secret vow that night that I would be more careful about such experiments in the future, and particularly careful about sharing them with others. For a long time after the debacle of the Terrible Tiramisu I made a point of restricting my public offerings to my two proven strengths to date: dancing and silence.

Amends for a Terrible Tiramisu

IT WAS SEVERAL years after the disastrous night of the Gorgonzola tiramisu before I could get back on the tiramisu wagon. I am happy to say that I now have a very simple, very fast, and very good tiramisu recipe that I execute with consistent success for all kinds of occasions. Also, happily, my friendship with all the Gruens has survived my culinary blunder. When Julia turned fifty, Luis and I went to her birthday party, hosted by Mimi Thompson and her husband, James Rosenquist, at their loft in TriBeCa. Julia's parents, Jane Wilson and John Gruen, in their eighties now but still going strong, were both there. Jane looked ravishing in a long dress, her eyes highlighted by that black eyeliner that was so stylish in the sixties and seventies. Jane is still painting, better than ever, and John has published yet another book—*Callas Kissed Me . . . Lenny Too.*

On that evening celebrating Julia's fiftieth, I was struck by how lucky I am to still share evenings with a grande dame like Jane and an artist like John and a dear friend like Jules. Family comes in many shapes and guises, and as I have said before, the Gruens will always have a special place in my heart as part of my New York family. May John's stories never stop coming; after all, he did kiss Callas—and Lenny too! And may all the Gruens forgive me for that evening when I stumbled into their lovely apartment carrying the terrible-smelling tiramisu.

Easy Peasy Tiramisu

SERVES 8

1½ cups very good brewed coffee, cooled

4 tablespoons rum

½ cup sugar

1 pound mascarpone cheese

2 teaspoons vanilla

24 ladyfingers

Very good dark chocolate

Unsweetened cocoa powder (for dusting on top)

Add the rum to the cooled coffee and set aside.

In a large bowl, with a handheld mixer, beat the sugar, mascarpone, and vanilla until creamy.

Place the ladyfingers on the bottom of a 3-quart dish and pour your spiked coffee over the ladyfingers. Spread your mascarpone mixture over the ladyfingers and shave a good amount of chocolate over the top of whole thing. Then dust with cocoa powder.

Chill in the fridge for at least two hours so everything gets settled.

See? Easy peasy!

CHAPTER NINE

So You Think You Can Dance?

To dance is to be out of yourself. Larger, more
beautiful, more powerful. This is power, it is glory on
earth, and it is yours for the taking.
—AGNES DE MILLE

My mother and I used to call each other whenever *Dancing with the Stars* was on during its first season. We would discuss the contestants and giggle and talk about everything and nothing at all. Recently I was sitting at home having dinner alone while I watched *So You Think You Can Dance?* and it made me miss her so much. What was even sadder was that I was brought to tears at least four times by the silly show. Even though it was not ballet, the passion I felt for the dancers as they performed was unimaginable.

I try to share my passion for dance with my students at the School of American Ballet. Dancing is not something that earns one millions, I tell them, and a dancer should never take advantage of or exploit his or her art. Whenever I see someone perform halfheartedly it makes me sad and embarrassed—imagine not having greater respect for the creative work you are representing, and for your audience, when every person in it has paid good money and put aside precious time, hoping to experience the transformative power of art.

Dancing is something that takes pure dedication and an unshakable belief in what you are doing—if you do not believe the story you are dancing, there is no way your audience is going to believe it. Achieving this takes so much more than you might think. As a dancer, every step you take must mean something. There can be no neutral gestures and no empty moments. When a dancer performs, he or she must do his or her best to bring beauty and intelligence and meaning to every moment in time. Every performance offers the possibility of new stories with new meanings, and as a dancer you can never exhaust these possibilities—you can always do something differently.

The infinite creative potential of dance has always thrilled me, and from a very early age the place where music and movement intersect has seemed a nearly mappable territory to me—a magical junction that offers precise and reliable entry to a separate realm where I can act with confidence and freedom. I discovered my first "dance doorway" to another realm when I was a toddler performing the hoop dance with my mother, and I have been searching for and exploring similar access points ever since. But in the days when I was a teenage rookie with the NYCB, I was using dance for more than artistic expression—I was using it as an emergency-escape route from the messy turmoil of my teenage insecurities and confusion. I leaped into the worlds that the marriage of music and movement created as a refuge from real life. Exploring the endless possibilities within a scripted ballet filled me with a heady sense of freedom and competence, and when a passage went well I could sense myself brushing up against something profound and mysterious and spiritual that was otherwise inaccessible to me. It was a thrilling, almost religious, sensation, and addictive in its own way.

I knew that there were other dancers who were technically better than I and physically more perfectly aligned. But I was a very natural dancer—things came easily and quickly to me, and when I danced well all the confidence I lacked in everyday life would come rushing through me with an explosive physical sensation that I can only compare to what I imagine flowers must feel when they bloom. I was ready to try anything anyone asked of me and I was willing to put in as many hours as necessary to get it right. After a while my intensity and focus paid off, and I was thrilled when, even as a first-year member of the corps, I began to get cast in a few solo and even lead roles.

Some of these early first roles—such as the pas de trois in Peter Martins's new ballet *Capriccio Italien* and another pas de trois in Jacques d'Amboise's *Irish Fantasy*—came to me through the normal casting process, and I was able to hone my performance through the standard method of countless rehearsals. Other opportunities came to me as the result of the double-edged nature of one of the ballet world's most dread demons: injury. Injury is a constant threat to all dancers, of course—but an injury to an established principal can turn into a lucky break for some lesser mortal who then gets to dance a role he would never otherwise have been cast in. Although these out-of-the-blue "lucky breaks" could be thrilling if they came your way, they were almost always extremely challenging and stressful, too. One of the most painful memories of my entire career came during my first year with the company, when Balanchine chose me as the last-minute emergency substitute to dance the "Gigue" solo in his ballet *Mozartiana*, after both Victor Castelli and Christopher d'Amboise were injured. When Rosemary Dunleavy explained to me that I had to learn the solo that afternoon and perform it that night, I just gulped. I was terrified, but I kept quiet and did as I was told, trying my best to tap into my talent for absorbing the steps in a few short hours.

When the moment of truth came that night, I ran out onstage in my costume and stood there, a little boy with long hair, smiling out at the audience—and then I completely blanked. I freaked out. I didn't know where I was or what I was doing. The conductor looked at me expectantly, and began. But I didn't move. I was completely alone onstage for the first time in my life, staring back at six thousand eyeballs. I felt like I was in a football stadium with everybody waiting for me to sing the national anthem. When the music kept going, I finally started kind of wiggling and hopping—and eventually I made my way to some semblance of what I had learned that afternoon. I was supposed to head offstage very slowly when I finally finished, turning and bowing to four ballerinas who had just made their entrance. It was so incredibly painful, and the moment I was finally offstage, I ran into the hallway and collapsed in a heap, convulsed with sobs and hyperventilating. Everyone around me kept telling me not to worry, nobody noticed, nobody noticed. But I knew this was not possible. And I felt completely humiliated. So much for what Kisselgoff had called my "magnificent stage presence." (If I ever want to really punish myself, I could probably go to the New York Public Library for the Performing Arts and dig up a film of that awful moment—and of many others as well. So far I haven't wanted to.) I went on to dance the "Gigue" solo of *Mozartiana* successfully many times in my career after that disastrous first attempt, but for dancers it is always the failures that come back again and again, in vivid Kodachrome detail.

Another unexpected challenge during that first year came when the company started rehearsals for Balanchine's holiday favorite, *The Nutcracker*. For my first "*Nuts*," as everyone in the company called the famous ballet, I was cast in the corps of the Spanish dance section called "Hot Chocolate," as a parent in the party scene, as a mouse in the fight scene—and as Mother Ginger. Mother Ginger may be a highlight for the children in the audience and for the other children who are dancing, but I have to say, the role is not a highlight for the boy who has to don the makeup and red wig and bonnet that make you look like a white Aunt Jemima on steroids, and then climb into a huge dress and walk onstage on stilts in drag. By the way—there is a big tambourine attached to the dress and you must carry a giant mirror and powder puff too. If you are not already humiliated enough, you soon will be as all of your colleagues begin either to snicker or give you that sad puppy-dog, wrinkled-eyebrow face. I remember thinking, "Boy, is this what I worked so hard for, to be a twelve-foot-tall drag queen?" But then I began to get into the role. By my fifth or sixth performance I had everyone in the wings cracking up so much I thought I might get myself fired.

Fortunately, I was given an opportunity to prove myself in a more serious role that winter season when Darci Kistler and I danced the leads in the company premiere of *Magic Flute*, the ballet Peter had choreographed on me and Katrina Killian for the school the previous year. I had been a last-minute (as in, day of the performance) choice to dance this same ballet with Darci for the annual gala performance only a few weeks earlier, after both Ib Andersen and Helgi Tomasson were injured—but shortly after I was chosen, Balanchine realized that at a major fund-raiser the audience members expected to see major stars. In a decision that was a big disappointment to me and a shock to Peter Martins, Balanchine changed his mind and informed Peter that he would have to dance his own ballet that night. "But I don't know it!" Peter had objected. "Well, dear, learn it," Balanchine had answered. "Do something, dear—make something up." That afternoon, instead of rehearsing to dance *Magic Flute* myself that evening, I helped Peter learn his own ballet. "You will get your ballet—don't worry," Peter had reassured me, and I was thrilled when he made good on his word and cast Darci and me for the company premiere of *Magic Flute*.

Afterward, Jennifer Dunning of the *New York Times* had nice things to say about the ballet and about me: "Mr. Soto, making his company debut as Luke on Saturday opposite a daredevil Darci Kistler, turned in a dream of a performance—all clear, easy classical line, beautifully finished multiple turns and an attack that had all the mingled buoyancy and gravity of youth. Still a teenager, Mr. Soto has impressive technical gifts. What is most remarkable, however, is that he never seems to push or strain for it, and dances with an unfailing sense of character. At times his manner was touchingly reminiscent of Mr. Martins."

Ms. Dunning was certainly right about one thing at least—I was enthralled with Peter, as a dancer, as a teacher, as a choreographer, and as a mentor in life in general. I was learning so much so quickly under his watchful eye, and it was thrilling to have a front-row seat as he explored and developed his own talents as a choreographer. Peter was a beautiful dancer, classically trained in Denmark in both ballet and pantomime, and his comments on even the simplest details—such as how one cupped one's hands over one's heart to express love—were revelatory to me. Peter also had (and has) an incredible musicality—meaning, he is blessed with a visceral and natural understanding of music, even in the most complex of scores—that helped me find and trust a certain native musicality in myself. I remember a story Peter once told me about an exchange he had with Balanchine when Balanchine was pressing him to choreograph a complicated passage of Stravinsky. Peter was unsure of himself and felt he lacked the musical sophistication that Balanchine, as an accomplished pianist and reader of music, could bring to the choreography for such a score. When he expressed his doubts to Balanchine, Mr. B replied, "Dear, you see—I can't trust my ears. I only trust my eyes—I have to look at the score. You are lucky—you just listen." At sixteen I did not have the training or the sophistication of a Peter Martins, and I would never have his classic tall, lean ballet physique. But I did share some measure of his natural musicality, and it gave the two of us a special shorthand form of communication when we worked together.

I was excited to feel this special relationship developing between Peter and me—he understood what I could do and he knew how to get me to do it. I understood what he wanted and sometimes even seemed to help him advance his vision further than he had expected. But despite this growing rapport, I was stunned when later that spring Peter called me into his office to tell me he had decided to choreograph a new ballet, *Concerto for Two Solo Pianos*, on Heather Watts and Ib Andersen and me. Ib Andersen was an established principal dancer and Heather was a star ballerina, both of them already dancing everything when I came to the company, and both of them my idols for some time. Heather's powerful and edgy presence onstage followed her into her private life—she had an aura that a dance critic once compared to "a dry martini," and a reputation for being a bit of a troublemaker. The rumor was that when she was at SAB the school had been on the verge of throwing her out because they couldn't handle her (she was always chewing gum or rebelling in some way) until Balanchine intervened and offered to take charge of her himself. He brought her into the company class, where he could keep an eye on her, and then he brought her into the company.

Heather and Peter had been romantically entwined for some time, in a high-voltage relationship that seemed always to be in its stormy season, and in 1978 Peter premiered his first ballet for the company, *Calcium Light Night*, with Heather and Daniel Duell as the leads. Peter's choreography in this ballet was startling—fresh and sharp edged and different, yet still within the Balanchine aesthetic—and Heather was stunning: a skinny, beautiful ballerina with long, long legs and gorgeous feet doing things that nobody had seen before.

Calcium became a huge success, and the first time I saw it I was amazed. I had allowed myself a private and far-fetched fantasy that someday I might dance this ballet with Heather. As a result I was more than a little excited when Peter chose me to work on his new ballet with Heather—but I was also terrified. I had worked with Peter as a choreographer in the school, but this ballet was being made for Balanchine's company, with plans for a premiere at a special Stravinsky Festival that June. Three thousand people would see the premiere. I had just turned seventeen.

Working with Peter and Heather on that ballet was one of my earliest and most intense lessons in the creative process of choreography—and, as such, unforgettable. Whenever we worked together I kept pretty quiet, but Heather and Peter seemed to have a language all their own—a hybrid of words and gestures and facial expressions that they delivered in quick shorthand bursts. Heather would stop in the middle of rehearsing a section of a duet with me, look at Peter, and say something like, "It feels itchy," or, "Hasn't this been done before?" Peter would nod, make a series of graceful motions with his hands and upper body, and say, "Try it backward. Slide." Heather would nod, turn to me, and dance the same beats in an entirely different, much better, way. Technically the music and the choreography in this new ballet of Peter's were very difficult, with many intricate notes and steps, and I remember thinking to myself—this is so incredibly *hard*, I can't believe I'm doing this. I will never forget one particularly awful moment in the rehearsal studio when I was holding Heather by both arms in an off-balance arabesque penchée and as she flipped to the front and fell into a split—as choreographed—I failed to catch her to break her fall. I couldn't believe it. I had just dropped this very famous ballerina right on . . . a very tender place. There was a horrible silence.

"What just happened?" Heather asked, the fury obvious in her voice.

"I—I don't know," I stammered. "I think maybe I'm a little groggy." There was another silence.

"Don't you ever, ever, *ever* drop a ballerina again," she scolded me. I was completely humiliated, but I took Heather's words to heart that day—and I did my very best to never, ever drop a ballerina again. Peter told me much later that Heather had been shocked when he first told her that for his new ballet he wanted to partner her with me—the youngest member of the corps de ballet—and she had resisted. "You've got to be kidding!" was her response. To which Peter in turn responded with a Balanchine story, about a famous prima ballerina who had refused to dance with a young dancer from the corps. Balanchine had turned to her and said, "My dear, one day he is going to be a major star and you will be begging to dance with him." Heather, always a gifted sparring partner, had replied, "Don't try to sell me that bullshit."

But almost immediately, as nervous and intimidated as I was in these early sessions with Peter and Heather, I could sense a special compatibility among the three of us. And in some ways my youth and inexperience helped to keep me from fully comprehending the daunting nature of what I was attempting. I just tried to do as I was told—and I paid careful attention to the music, trying to keep track of everything and get through the steps. We worked for weeks in a studio with the two brilliant pianists Gordon Boelzner and Jerry Zimmerman, translating the musicians' counts into our dance beats, and painstakingly memorizing the intricate movements and structure of the ballet. Peter's choreography in this ballet was much more complex and demanding than anything I had danced before and we developed nicknames to use as signposts for different passages—"Pac-Man" referred to a moment when all the corps dancers begin to peel off-stage, following one another like a line of hungry Pac-Man monsters. I knew these intricate steps were not something my body could quickly absorb, and that I would have to count everything very carefully on each run-through, but whenever I could I also tried my very best to give something extra, to try to make the performance bravura—it *had* to be something special. I was performing with the famous Heather Watts and the equally famous Ib Andersen, but I was a lowly member of the corps. If the audience didn't applaud at the premiere, I fretted privately, it would obviously be *my* fault.

On the day *Concerto for Two Solo Pianos* premiered at the Stravinsky Festival I was a nervous wreck, but I did my best and I thought we had got through it well. After the performance, Peter came to me backstage, obviously not happy. "Why did you mark?" he asked me. "To mark" is the choreographer's term for when a dancer fails to dance a ballet full out, and therefore "marks" the ballet. I was horrified. "I didn't mark," I countered. I had danced as full out as I trusted myself to at the time—trying so hard to please Peter, to not drop Heather, and to come up to Ib Andersen's high level as an artist—but it hadn't been enough. "You cannot mark this ballet—you have to go super full out,"

Peter said angrily. I went upstairs and dressed and left the theater, feeling terrible.

Fortunately Peter's ballet was a success with the critics, and was praised for its "cerebral complexity." I made a point of getting sharper and pushing past my lack of confidence, going "super full out," as Peter had said, in the next performances. Peter complimented my efforts and I didn't have to kill myself after all. A few nights later I cleared another potentially humiliating challenge when I replaced an injured Victor Castelli and successfully partnered Judith Fugate in the fourth movement of Balanchine's *Symphony in C*. Evidently Balanchine, who was very sick and in the hospital at the time, had chosen me, saying he wanted "the dark one with the black hair."

My incredible good luck in roles continued in the winter season of 1983 as I partnered Heather in *Magic Flute* (after Ib Andersen was injured) and in another season of *Concerto for Two Solo Pianos*, and danced a solo in the premiere of Jacques d'Amboise's ballet *Celebration*. It felt like an almost surreal upward trajectory, and I was anxious, sure that it had to end—and sure enough it did. Peter was bringing a new ballet he had choreographed for the school, *Delibes Divertissement*, to the company, with Heather and me dancing the lead parts. It was a pretty ballet set to excerpts from Léo Delibes's *Sylvia*, and in February we danced the premiere. I felt pretty good about our performance—we had learned our parts well, and we had danced expressively. But then I saw the papers. "A NIGHT TO FORGET" was the headline the *New York Post* ran over a picture of Heather and me standing center stage with huge, triumphant grins on our faces. In his review

Clive Barnes slammed the ballet. Another stinging dismissal came from Jack Anderson in the *New York Times*: "The choreography's delicacy did not seem suited to Miss Watts' forthright style and Mr. Soto did not yet look at home in the most demanding passages. . . . Mr. Martins has done little more than take some music and cover it with nicely patterned choreographic linoleum." I had just had my first brutal lesson in the devastating effect dance critics can have when they decide to give the thumbs-down. In retrospect, I think the critics' savagery at this particular moment may have marked the beginning of their negative attitude toward the possibility that Peter might take over the company someday. Balanchine was very sick, and everyone knew it.

It was a dark spring in general that year. I was down on myself because of these negative reviews, and the communal morale of NYCB was down because of Balanchine's degenerating health. On April 30, our company—and indeed the whole dance world—was saddened when Balanchine died. Ulrik and I were in our Eighteenth Street apartment when we got the call with the sad news early Saturday morning. I had to head to the theater to rehearse Balanchine's *Kammermusik No. 2* for a matinee performance—I was actually replacing Ulrik, who had been injured—and by performance time that afternoon the theater was mobbed with people who had come to honor Balanchine by watching his company dance. I was off that evening, but I came back to the theater to watch Peter Martins and Suzanne Farrell dance the second movement of Balanchine's *Symphony in C*. Before the movement began I was so nervous—Peter and Suzanne and Balanchine had such a history together, built on so much respect and shared vision. Would Peter and Suzanne be able to dance? As the adagio, which I would dance many times myself in later years, began, Peter led Suzanne onto the stage. My heart was pounding as one of the most beautiful visions I have ever witnessed unfolded onstage. Peter was absolutely brilliant as a partner, and Suzanne was magical, floating through the ballet with the most ethereal grace. Everyone in the audience was mesmerized, and when the performance finally came to an end, there were two beats of the deepest possible silence, followed by an explosion of applause and emotion in the packed theater.

On May 4, at the Russian Orthodox Cathedral of Our Lady of the Sign, on East Ninety-third Street, I stood in the pouring rain with the masses of mourners who had lined up to file past Balanchine's open coffin. I remember thinking how strange it was that such a unique and powerful force could really come to an end. Would Mr. B choreograph the angels in heaven? The question made me think of the final composition he had choreographed for the Tchaikovsky Festival in 1981, the *Pathétique*. It was an amazing scene in which all the ballerinas stood in the background wearing enormous ten-foot wings while all the men in the company filed onto the stage in monks' robes and then spread out to make what eventually revealed itself to be the formation of a cross. The men in the cross formation were all positioned at gradually descending levels, standing at the back of the stage and lying on their stomachs in the front, so the cross seemed to be tipped toward the audience in a semiupright position, and once everyone was in place the men began doing push-ups and other coordinated movements to make the cross appear to "breathe." A breathing cross! Who but Balanchine would ever imagine such a scene, let alone create it? I remember it was such a breathtaking vision, such an amazing moment, and at the time I was shocked that the audience seemed to roll right past it, as if it was just too wild and beautiful and moving a thing to acknowledge.

I was standing in line that day near choreographer and co–ballet master John Taras, and when I reached Balanchine's open coffin, John kept saying to me, "Kiss him, Jock. Kiss him." Kiss him? Kiss a dead man? No. I had the deepest respect for Balanchine, but I wasn't about to kiss him. I had no desire to kiss his deadness, and, frankly, I could not believe he would want me to. As I filed past, crossing myself the way my mother had taught me, I said a silent prayer for him and a thank-you and good-bye to the man who had helped deliver to me my dream. But kiss him as he lay there? No. My kiss to Balanchine would be to remember him always, to remember what he had taught me, and to try always to be an honest and open performer—to "just dance."

The City Ballet has as fierce a show-must-go-on ethic as I have ever seen, and after Balanchine's death all of us in the company picked up and threw ourselves into the process of continuing and trying to expand his legacy. That spring, choreographer and co–ballet master Jerome Robbins premiered his new ballet *Glass Pieces*. I was dancing as a member of the corps ensemble, and during rehearsals Robbins chose me to be the first runner in a string of male joggers who rush onstage to the dramatic pounding of drums. I have always suspected that it may have been my Native American looks rather than any particular talent that caught Jerry's eye and prompted him to choose me as the lead runner. But I was happy to be noticed by him at all.

It was exciting to be getting so many roles as such a young member of the company, but I was about to learn about one of the downsides—specifically, the hazards of juggling two demanding roles with two demanding choreographers at the same time. Peter had chosen me to partner Maria Calegari in Balanchine's *Symphony in Three Movements*—a role debut for me—at about the same time that Helgi Tomasson had cast me as one of five soloist boys in a new ballet he was choreographing, called *Ballet d'Isoline*. The rehearsals for each of these ballets were intense, and often back-to-back, and when Helgi kept us late one day to do some last-minute revisions on his ballet he caught me eyeing the clock nervously and muttering something under my breath. He was furious. When I explained that I was overdue to rehearse *Symphony in Three Movements* for my role debut that night, he became even more furious. "Get out of this room, and out of my ballet," he screamed. He just kicked me right out of his ballet, on the spot!

I was devastated, and I arrived at my rehearsal for *Symphony in Three Movements* a blubbering wreck. I was so upset I couldn't dance. My career was over, I explained to Peter and ballet mistress Rosemary Dunleavy between my sobs. I had pissed Helgi off—really, really pissed him off—and he had kicked me out of his ballet.

Peter and Rosemary looked at each other and then both tried to calm me. "Let it go," they said. "Everything will be okay. Just let it go." At that moment it seemed impossible that I would ever recover from the incident—professionally or personally. But of course I did—and rather quickly. I danced my debut in *Symphony in Three Movements* with Maria that night, and danced it well. The *New York Times* compared my "projection of volume" to that of Edward Villella and then added: "Mr. Soto made every small step important." The praise did wonders to soothe my upset feelings at being booted from Helgi's ballet, and as I lifted my chin and turned my back on the matter, a part of me—the rejected part—withdrew and grew a protective layer of tough skin. I was learning one of the most crucial skills for any professional dancer: you can get upset, but never let it show.

For everyone at the New York City Ballet the work ethic was always incredibly intense—we were dancing, dancing, dancing from the moment we got up until the final curtain at 11 p.m. But along with this hard work there was plenty of play, and at times life felt impossibly exotic to me. The performances were quite magical in themselves, and over the course of each year there was also the thrill of being part of a roving gypsy band that moved en masse from place to place. That July we went to Saratoga for our annual summer session, and that August the entire company boarded a European-bound jet for a foreign tour that would include two weeks each in London, Copenhagen, and Paris. Our collective spirits were soaring as we took off, and the seven-hour flight that followed was like a cross between the movies *Airplane* and *Animal House*—I remember about two-thirds of the way through our journey the flight attendant got on the intercom and announced: "Will the New York City Ballet *please* get back in their seats and remain quiet for the remainder of the flight?"

It was my first European tour with the company, and it was wonderful. We danced our way across the stages of Europe, and when we weren't dancing we ate and drank our way through each city we visited. I was trying to keep up with Ulrik and our friends, all of whom were so much more experienced and well traveled than I, and one night in Paris my insecurities about myself and about Ulrik's affections got to me and I lost my composure. We were at a black-tie party for the company that was hosted at the famous restaurant Maxim's, and I was sipping a glass of white wine while chatting with a dancer named Liz. When I looked across the room, I saw Ulrik and another dancer sitting on a sofa in quiet conversation, and it was instantly clear to me that something was going on between them. Jealousy and fury rose volcanically inside me. I handed my wine to Liz, strode across the room, and, without saying a word, turned the sofa holding the two-timing Ulrik and the offending dancer upside down. Then I stomped off into the Paris night. It was a pretty adolescent performance on my part—but then, I was an adolescent. And, true to my age, I quickly forgot about the upset, and Ulrik and I sailed on through the rest of the trip as if nothing had happened.

Back in New York for the fall season after our European tour, we all hit the ground running and I had little time to brood over Ulrik's possible infidelity. A big thrill came when I was asked to replace the injured Bart Cook and partner Heather in the "Rubies" section of Balanchine's *Jewels*—the very same passage of the ballet that had caught my eye on *The Ed Sullivan Show* so many years ago. Every time I see *Jewels* it amazes me that Balanchine could build such energy and movement and intense emotion into a ballet that has no story line proper, and could use the abstract concept of three different precious stones to express so much about life and dance. That fall I also partnered Heather in the second movement of *Symphony in C* for the first time, and when *Nutcracker* season rolled around I was cast as the Leading Hot Chocolate. "Leading Hot Chocolate" is not something many people would put on a résumé, but in our little world inside Balanchine's infinite world, every step you took was important.

Nutcracker season that year was significant for everyone in the company for another reason. On the night that marked the one hundredth performance of Balanchine's ballet, we all watched Peter Martins give his final performance as a dancer, as the Cavalier to Suzanne Farrell's Sugar Plum Fairy. I remember it was such an emotional moment, standing backstage after the performance, waiting to go to Peter's retirement party, dressed in my tuxedo with my little snap-on bow tie. Peter was a beautiful dancer, and we were never going to see him dance again. He was still young—it seemed almost criminal. But with Balanchine gone, Peter was just too busy to dance. I couldn't imagine not dancing, and as I glanced over at Peter, wondering how he could possibly be handling this, I saw that he was laughing. "Did you see that?" he asked, with a big grin. "Jesus! I had to save Suzanne from that crazy turn! Did you see?" Watching him, you would never have guessed that there was anything unusual about this particular night, or that anything special was going on about which he might have cared. As usual, Peter was the ultimate professional—a smooth, self-effacing, disciplined performer, just one of many participants in a seamless presentation of art. I thought for a moment about the day when my own retirement would eventually come and wondered if I would be able to handle myself with as much dignity and grace. But that horrifying, almost unthinkable event seemed impossibly far away—would I even live long enough to see it? Best not to think about such things, I told myself, as I straightened my tie and headed off to Peter's party. Best to just dance.

A Soto Variation on a
Balanchine Classic

BALANCHINE'S DEATH IN 1983 was a terrible loss for the whole world, and over the years there have been many ways in which his admirers have honored his memory. I heard a new one recently when retired NYCB-dancer Karin von Aroldingen told me that she keeps a piece of Balanchine's last birthday cake in her freezer and eats a little bite of it each year on his birthday. Karin described how she, Mr. B, and Mr. B's fourth wife, Tanaquil le Clercq, would often cook meals together, and she kindly lent me a copy of *The Ballet Cook Book*, a compendium of recipes from famous dancers that Tanny put together in 1966.

In her book Tanny opens the section that presents her husband's recipes with his description of his ideal sandwich: "Take one half of an un-toasted Thomas' English muffin, cover it generously with sweet butter, say about a quarter of an inch, spread a layer of excellent black caviar over the butter, at *least* one inch thick, and cover with the other half of the muffin. If you can't afford lots of caviar, better to forget the whole thing."

Reading about Mr. Balanchine's special caviar sandwich made me hungry for an alternate version—a more affordable (and less caloric) item than Balanchine's, on a bagel instead of an English muffin—that Luis and I often have as a treat on New Year's Day. One evening as Luis and I were enjoying our caviar-topped bagels and browsing through *The Ballet Cook Book*, we flipped to the book's inside front cover and discovered an inscription, from Tanny to Mr. B: "Christmas 1967 To George—with all my love, and gratitude for helping me so much with this book. T." We gasped. It was thrilling to imagine that on a Christmas Day long ago, Tanaquil le Clercq presented her husband, George Balanchine, with this very book. I wonder what they ate for dinner that night.

New Year's Day Bagel-and-Caviar Treat

SERVES 1 SELFISH, GREEDY PERSON

This sublime sandwich needn't be reserved for New Year's Day. I once tore my calf during a rehearsal and came home in one of those hideous boots that makes you look like you have injured yourself beyond repair. I was quite upset, because it felt like it was about the one hundredth time this had happened. As I lay in bed, feeling sorry for myself, Luis surprised me with this gorgeous delight.

1 sesame bagel, toasted   *Red onion slices*

Cream cheese   *Caviar!*

Lox

Toast your bagel, and then spread cream cheese on it. Layer on your lox and red onion slices. Then top it with as much caviar as possible.

If someone asks for a bite, refuse, saying, "Go get your own, buddy!" A nice glass of Veuve Clicquot is a must. Cheers!

CHAPTER TEN

The Enigma of Arrival

*Success is liking yourself, liking what you do,
and liking how you do it.*
—MAYA ANGELOU

When I think back on my first decade of living alone in New York, I am saddened to realize how little I saw or even talked to members of my family during those years. I had thrown myself into my dancing and embraced my life with my new NYCB family with a single-minded intensity, and there were long periods when I didn't even know where my parents and my brother were living. Communication between us was complicated by the fact that they were still constantly on the move—I vaguely remember my parents living in various locations in California, Arizona, New Mexico, Florida, and Texas during this period—as well as by the hit-or-miss nature of pay-phone-to-pay-phone calls in a pre–cell phone era. Neither I nor my parents could afford the cost of plane tickets for visits, and in my case a performance schedule made any non-work-related travel impossible anyway. Even the traditional holidays like Thanksgiving and Christmas were off-limits.

I do remember when my brother enlisted in the navy in 1981, at age eighteen, and was stationed in Guam for four years. Kiko and I have since joked about the fact that in what he intended as an act of rebellion during his "I hate my father" period, Kiko wound up doing exactly what our father, angry with *his* father, had done at about the same age. In 1986, Kiko got married to his first wife in San Diego. I hadn't seen Kiko since my family had left me in New York, but I still could not make it to the wedding. My nephew Bryce was born in March of 1987—and it was I who suggested his name, inspired by my friend the painter Brice Marden, though Kiko revised the spelling slightly. It wasn't until 1991, when I was dancing in San Diego, that I finally got to enjoy a brief visit with Kiko and meet his son Bryce and his wife, who was pregnant again. My nephew Trevor was born that July. Sadly, these are the only major family milestones that I can identify for that decade.

The physical distance between my family and me during these years was compounded, of course, by the widening gap between the kinds of lives we were leading. I was, by this time, a fully launched young homosexual, living my life on my own terms in Manhattan. I had never discussed my sexuality with my parents, and I had no desire to do so. Our worlds were just too different, and I knew my father, at least, would certainly not want to have that conversation. During my infrequent and brief telephone conversations with my parents I carefully steered clear of any discussion of my personal life. This was easy enough with my father, since our talks usually lasted a maximum of ten seconds. In conversations with my mother, both of us were careful to stick to safe topics—I'd tell her what I was dancing and she would give me a basic update on family members. When I got off the phone I would heave a sigh of relief, happy to know that I had dodged any exchange of real information with my parents and could now return to my emotionally charged but repressed and uncommunicative life with my two-timing older boyfriend and my round-the-clock adventures with my exotic, dysfunctional surrogate family in New York.

Thinking back, I sometimes wonder how any of us managed to survive that period of our lives. We were all so young, and our lives were unfolding at such a fast and relentless pace, seesawing between two very different worlds in a strange counterpoint of discipline and dissolution. My hours and hours of daily rehearsals and high-pressure evening performances for NYCB all fell within the beautiful, precise, polished, classical lines of Balanchine's world; when we had finished performing and finally exited the "Philip Johnson Cave," as we sometimes called the New York State Theater, my fellow dancers and I would throw ourselves with equal intensity into our entirely unchoreographed rampages through the dark underworld of the 1980s late-night club scene in New York.

Heather and I had been dancing together more and more and getting closer and closer as time passed, both on- and offstage, and often she and I would head out into the night together with Ulrik and Peter and a few other good friends. We would usually begin with a dinner somewhere, and then those who felt sufficiently restless and hell-bent would

continue on, roving from club to club or party to party, gulp-
ing vodka and smoking cigarettes and falling in and out of
myriad small dramas and flirtations and fights.

By this time, Heather and Peter, at least in my mind, had
taken on the specific role of surrogate parents within my surrogate family—in fact, to this day Peter refers to me as his
"second son," an honorary status I am so touched and grateful to have been given. But even surrogate families have their
rough times, and I have memories of many uncomfortable
evenings when I would sit silently through dinner, my stom-
ach in a tense knot, as tempers flared and harsh words flew
back and forth across the table. Another source of pain for
me during this period was my gradual realization that Ulrik,
with whom I was still very much in love, definitely was not
the most faithful of lovers. I'm sure my suspicions and my
anger about Ulrik's infidelities were magnified by the innocence and vulnerability of my relative youth, but at the time
all I knew was that it hurt. Despite my pain, I couldn't bring
myself to confront Ulrik directly. (Was this perhaps a behavior I had learned from my mother? At least I wasn't clipping
his toenails for him before he went out to cheat on me!) Instead, I kept quiet and let everything build up inside me. For
the most part, I managed to keep my composure, at least in
public, but on occasion my feelings would flare up suddenly,
as they had in Paris, and I would find myself doing strange
things I could never have predicted and that still surprise me
when I think of them today.

I remember sitting at a club called the Boy Bar late one
night, next to the same dancer whom I had suspected was
having an affair with Ulrik in Paris. When I saw the two of

them exchange a quick and meaningful glance, it cut me to the quick. Unfortunately, the method I chose to vent my hurt and anger was a little odd: I took the big wad of gum I was chewing and parked it in the offending dancer's hair. (I'm sure that showed him.) When the dancer demanded that I remove the gum, I grabbed the bartender's lemon-slicing knife and—after making sure the gum was imbedded in as much hair as possible—hacked away to remove the mess. Ten minutes later, when this newly coiffed dancer and I passed each other on the way to the men's room at the back of the bar, I rounded out my odd retaliation tactics by grabbing him and kissing him.

Displays of this sort were juvenile and illogical on my part, a cuckoo jumble of reactive actions. But I didn't know how else to express my pain and confusion. In fact, if my physical life in those early years was an odd shuttle between the discipline of dancing and the dissolution of night-crawls, my emotional life was an equally bizarre back-and-forth between expression and repression. Onstage I focused on pouring as much artistic feeling and emotion and passion as I could muster into every step I took, while offstage I worked just as hard to conceal my true feelings from everyone around me—including myself.

Another aspect of life back then that amazes and even frightens me when I think about it was the total absence of limits or rules on social and sexual behavior in the early 1980s. There was very little public understanding or awareness of AIDS as yet, and life and love and plain old sex were pursued with a happy and reckless abandon. Everybody was sleeping with everybody, it sometimes seemed to me. There were company members who would switch-hit, back and forth, in their sexual preferences (I remember there was a psychic who was popular with many of the dancers who seemed to be particularly adept at convincing gay people that they were straight, and vice versa), thereby compounding the possible permutations and combinations in life. I probably would have considered jumping into the joyous fray with more enthusiasm myself if I had had a little more free time, had been a little surer of my own looks, and had not been such a hopeless romantic. Luckily for me, perhaps, I was what I was: extremely busy, very shy, somewhat insecure about my looks, just a little old-fashioned about love—and very definitely 100 percent gay. Focusing on my dancing and trying to keep track of my wandering boyfriend kept me pretty busy, and as a result I got into less trouble than I might have otherwise.

In an interview my mother once commented about this period of my life, and what she considered the miracle of my survival as a young teenager on my own in New York: "It wasn't until later that we thought about what we had done— leaving such a young boy alone in the city—and we were horrified. We really regretted it. I don't know how he made it through, how he managed not to tumble into some kind of terrible trouble." It's true that I did not have the traditional structure of family or an educational institution to guide me, but in my professional life I was surrounded by amazing role models. Everyone involved with the company—the brilliant teachers and choreographers and dancers, the stage managers and crew, the talented set and costume designers, the artisans in the NYCB costume shop, and, of course, the members of the wonderful NYCB Orchestra—was driven by and devoted to their art. And I was right there with them: driven and devoted, delighted and honored to be working with like-minded people who had so much to teach me.

In the winter season of 1984 an important new influence on my dance career began when Jerome Robbins, who always sat in the audience, watching every ballet performance, began to notice me and started to use me more. In January he gave me a role debut in his *Goldberg Variations*, partnering Stephanie Saland in the second "orange" pas de deux in the final section, and another role debut dancing with Maria Calegari in his *I'm Old-Fashioned*. Jerry's ballets were always challenging, abstract and lyrical and romantic all at once, and he was incredibly demanding about their technical execution. Every moment had to be perfect, and in rehearsals we sometimes couldn't get through more than a few measures of the score in an hour's time. It was exhausting, and his manner was intimidating—fierce and gruff and downright mean at times. But at the same time Jerry had an intuition for the special qualities certain dancers might have within themselves, and he was generous about giving dancers plenty of room to find those qualities and bring something new to a performance. I was thrilled when a little later that season Jerry cast me as the Boy in Brick in his very beautiful ballet *Dances at a Gathering*, and then cast me and Diana White in the lead roles of *Moves*—his unusual ballet performed in silence, without any music—when he decided to bring it to the company for the first time.

The pace of all this was a little dizzying. That same season I was also partnering Lourdes Lopez in Balanchine's *Western Symphony*, dancing my debut in the first pas de trois in *Agon*, and partnering Nichol Hlinka in the premiere of a new Peter Martins ballet, *A Schubertiad*. Lourdes is of Cuban descent and has a strong and regal presence, and she and I made a dark and exotic duo onstage. (Someone once said Lourdes made me look "more American.") Off-stage, Lourdes and I were good friends and shared a similar sense of humor. I remember one afternoon, after a particu-larly frustrating rehearsal with Jerry, Lourdes and I found ourselves sitting alone onstage in the New York State The-ater, exhausted and upset. We looked at each other, and a split second later we both started screaming at the top of our lungs. We continued screaming for five full minutes, until finally, fully purged, we dissolved into laughter. Lourdes was a brilliant and very dramatic dancer (who can forget the drama of her beautiful black hair and the vibrant red tutu in *Firebird*?) and we seemed especially well suited as part-ners in *Western Symphony*—although it's kind of funny if you think about it: a Hispanic-Indian guy with a Cuban girl dancing a Russian choreographer's ballet about the Ameri-can Wild West. But this is the beauty of ballet—it can draw inspiration from the most unexpected sources and can com-bine the most unlikely elements into a work of beauty.

I was sure I didn't deserve all of these plum roles with such brilliant ballerinas, and I knew that soon enough someone else would figure this out too. But in the meantime I decided to keep quiet, and keep learning as much as possible. I was getting a crash course in the intricate art of partnering in gen-eral, and valuable exposure to the different quirks and styles of so many talented ballerinas. It was fascinating. Some danc-ers had precise feet and beautiful hands, some had amazing strength, some brought a special intimacy of touch—the variations and subtleties seemed endless. The most basic rules of partnering had come to me very naturally, and are the same basics I try to teach my students now—like making sure you lift with your legs and thighs. If you rely only on your back, you'll kill your career. Or how to hold and how not to hold: I tell my students that when you take a ballerina by the wrists it shouldn't look like you are riding a motorcycle. Never paddle a ballerina in a turn—that is, do not slap at her waist to move her along in her turn. Stir her discreetly with your finger in finger turns, not like you have a spoon and she is a pot of soup. When you are standing behind a ballerina you shouldn't be noticed; stay inconspicuous, keep your hands as quiet and hidden as possible. Be her invisible shock absorber as she lands, her invisible engine as she takes off. Everything is about your ballerina, and you are there to enable her magic. And, perhaps most important, never try to "act" your role—if you act it you ruin it. Just dance it.

As I became a more seasoned dancer I also began to understand the complex relationship between performers and their audience, and I learned that a ballet can have a strange life cycle of its own, falling in and out of favor with the audience and with the critics for what are sometimes very mysterious reasons. The critics in particular, I began to feel, could drive you crazy if you paid too much attention to them. When Heather and I premiered Peter's *Concerto for Two Solo Pianos* in 1982 the critics had praised its "tart astringency" and "jazzy and mysterious" qualities, but in 1984 when we danced the same ballet they were impatient with its intricacies, and they called it "a relentless succession of steps."

They couldn't decide if there was anything they liked about *A Schubertiad* either, and they blew hot and cold on Robbins's *Moves*. I came to the conclusion that it would be best if I ignored all this commentary and analysis and just danced the ballets for themselves, as I always had before anyone started commenting on my performances. I continued to throw everything I could into my dancing each night, and when the curtains closed for the last time I ducked out the backstage door and disappeared into the blissful noise and anonymity of New York City. Once again, my life was polarizing itself in a strange way as I alternated between my hours of wanting to be closely watched and admired onstage, and my hours of wanting to be invisible and ignored while offstage.

During this period I became so adept at blocking out all comments about my dancing except those that came from teachers in a classroom or choreographers in rehearsals, that I was taken by surprise when Peter called me into his office in June 1984 and told me that I was being promoted from the corps de ballet to a soloist. Melinda Roy (who remains one of my closest friends to this day), Helene Alexopoulos, David Moore, and I were all being promoted to soloists, and Lourdes Lopez and Stephanie Saland and Joseph Duell were all being promoted to principals. I was so happy, and I couldn't believe my life could be this perfect—that I, at age nineteen, was being given this promotion and the opportunity to pursue the one thing I had always wanted to pursue. After my promotion I began attacking my roles with a new confidence, and when the *Nutcracker* season rolled around that year, I danced as Cavalier to Heather's Sugar Plum Fairy. In her end-of-the-year wrap-up on dance for the *New York*

Times, Anna Kisselgoff wrote, "Jock Soto should be singled out for literally everything this very talented dancer did in the New York City Ballet." Hey, now this was the kind of criticism I was willing to read!

In the months that followed I got to dance exciting role debuts in a number of ballets—including Balanchine's *Bugaku*, *Midsummer Night's Dream*, *Brahms-Schoenberg Quartet*, and *Cortège Hongrois*, and Robbins's *In the Night* and *Opus 19/The Dreamer*—and I allowed myself to bump up a notch in confidence. Instead of a *would-be*, I felt I could now consider myself an *up-and-coming* ballet dancer. But it seems that the moment we drop our guard even an inch is always the moment we fall—and my behavior after being promoted to a soloist with Balanchine's company dropped right into this clichéd trap. I felt more secure and accomplished as a dancer than I ever had before, and yet I also violated the number one rule for any dancer—and particularly for me, as a dancer with a "more solid" build: I let myself get fat. Over the course of only a few months I went from 175 to 190 pounds.

In the past I have asked myself how I could have let this happen at such a critical point in my career—was I depressed or unhappy or confused? I did have a few complaints but, with the exception of Ulrik's ongoing infidelities, most of them were pretty minor. It was annoying that my dressing room, which I shared with four other soloists, was in a part of the theater that was so far from the stage we called it New Jersey. I was frustrated when, for a period just after my promotion to soloist, it seemed the only ballet I was dancing was *Moves*—the Robbins ballet that is danced in total silence. But as I look back now it seems quite obvious that the biggest reason for my sudden weight gain had to be the sudden decrease in daily demands (and resulting boredom and free time) that came with being a soloist in those days. At the time of my promotion the rule was that soloists danced solo roles (when so cast) and did not dance with the corps. (This is no longer the case— soloists these days do dance some corps roles.) The result was that back then as a soloist you often performed much less frequently—sometimes only once or twice a week—than if you were in the corps or if you were a principal. Unless you kept after yourself and made it a point to attend a lot of classes, you could wind up sitting around a lot—which is what I did. Then, of course, I was making a little more money as a soloist, so I could also afford to eat better and go to more restaurants. Finally, because I had more leisurely mornings, I began cooking myself the big breakfasts my mother always used to serve me as a child. I perfected my execution of her famous Biscuits 'n' Gravy, Baked Bacon, and Cheesy Frittata recipes.

Not only did I get fat but I also managed to keep myself in complete denial about my expanding silhouette. But one day I was summoned to Peter's office, and after I sat down he looked at me in a strange way. He took a deep breath and told me that he had decided to promote Christopher d'Amboise from soloist to principal. I felt a tiny little stab of competitive jealously when I heard this news, but only for a second and I didn't say anything. Peter looked at me strangely again, hesitating slightly, and then he blurted it out: "I was going to promote you as well, Jock. But I . . . I . . . I just can't. You're too *fat*. You can't dance like that!" He gestured toward my even-more-solid-than-usual self.

I'm sure all the blood must have drained from my face on the spot at that moment. The second Peter uttered that dread three-letter word, I knew that it was true. Suddenly I was aware of the soft layer of pudginess encasing my torso. I was horrified and humiliated and very angry with myself. How had I let such a thing happen? How could I have let myself screw up like this? Here I had worked so hard to get myself launched on my life's dream, dancing with the best ballet dancers in the world in the best ballet company in the world, and then I had just waddled right up to the feed trough and let myself get fat!

Disgusted with myself and determined to reform, I was on a diet before I even walked out of Peter's office. I put myself on a very strict program—eating mostly yogurt and nuts—and started going to restaurants less often and working out more aggressively. Two weeks later I had lost the fifteen pounds of gained weight, but I had not yet regained my confidence and dignity. I was still furious with myself for screwing up in such a stupid manner, but what could I do? I had blown it.

Sometimes I tell myself that one of the reasons I gained weight in this period was not just the restaurant food and big breakfasts, but also that I had been getting more and more interested in cooking, and more ambitious and confident about what I attempted in the kitchen. It's true that even after I put myself on a strict diet I still enjoyed cooking a nice meal for others—in fact, at times this almost felt like a substitute for eating. One Friday night only a few weeks after Peter had hit me with the gruesome truth about my weight, I decided to prepare a feast for Ulrik and Peter and Heather at the apartment where Ulrik and I were living at the time. I decided I would make a very grown-up meal—the famous pork roast recipe, with all the trimmings, that I had learned from Jane Wilson (Julia Gruen's mother). Heather and I had started cooking together a lot—it was a kind of secondary offstage partnership that we had discovered and enjoyed—and she had come over early to help me. As we gossiped and chopped in the kitchen she kept teasing me.

"I've got a secret, I've got a secret," she kept saying, those intense blue eyes of hers dancing with mischief. "What?" I kept asking, but she refused to share. When the doorbell rang a little later, Heather insisted that I go answer it, even though I was at a crucial point in my kitchen duties. Slightly disgruntled, I walked over and threw open the front door. There stood Ulrik and Peter, wearing huge smiles and holding a magnum of Dom Pérignon.

"Congratulations, Jock! You've been promoted!" Peter shouted as he thrust the champagne toward me and then gave me a big hug.

I was stunned. I had moved to New York City seven years earlier at age thirteen to pursue my ballet dream, and now it seemed possible I might actually get a chance to climb the ranks and prove myself with the best of them. At age twenty, I had just become the youngest principal dancer with the New York City Ballet.

On that night when I was promoted to the status of principal dancer, Heather and Peter and Ulrik and I opened that big bottle of Dom Pérignon and drank every drop as we celebrated my happiness. I am sure we also must have sat down at some point to eat the dinner Heather and I had prepared, but I have no recollection of our meal after the initial toasts. From the moment Peter delivered his exciting news, I was elsewhere—floating about in a happy, far-off place I think they sometimes call cloud nine.

Years later, when Heather and I began working together on a cookbook containing some of our favorite meals, we decided to include our version of the recipe we served that evening. We christened it "Principal Pork," and to this day it remains one of my favorite meals for celebrating milestone moments.

A Feast for Milestone Moments

FOR YEARS I served the pork roast Heather and I dubbed Principal Pork as a special entrée for special occasions. The recipe involves taking a three-pound boned pork loin and rubbing it with cumin, fresh thyme, and minced garlic; then tying the roast into a long log and rubbing it with olive oil; and finally placing it in a roasting pan with a half cup each of orange juice and red wine, popping it in a preheated 350-degree oven, and cooking it for about an hour, or until a meat thermometer reads 160 degrees. Nothing could be simpler, right?

Well, how about a pork roast that you stick in a Crock-Pot in the morning, then go off to work and forget about for the rest of the day? The following *barbacoa* recipe offers a delightful Mexican twist (courtesy of Luis) on the more traditional pork roast. Your whole building will be jealous of the gorgeous smell wafting from your apartment all day. Serve it with corn tortillas (you can warm them in the microwave), rice and beans, green and red salsa, and the spicy guacamole on page 166. You will be in pig heaven!

A Mexican Twist on Principal Pork, or Slow-Cooked Barbacoa à la Luis

SERVES 8 TO 10

THE MARINADE:

2 ounces ancho chilies

4 ounces guajillo chilies

8 cloves garlic

½ small onion

3 sprigs fresh thyme

1 tablespoon dried
   Mexican oregano

1 tablespoon black
   peppercorns

3 tablespoons salt

4 fresh bay leaves

2 tablespoons white wine
   vinegar

Juice of 1 large orange

THE ROAST:

5 pounds pork butt,
   bone in

18 dried avocado leaves
   (available at Mexican
   groceries or online)

12 fresh bay leaves

Half a bottle of your
   favorite Mexican beer
   (Tecate or Modelo, for
   example)

NOTE: Before you do anything, make sure the pork butt fits inside your Crock-Pot. If you have a small Crock-Pot, you may want to use a 4-pound boneless pork butt cut into 2 or 3 pieces.

Remove all the seeds and veins from the chilies. Boil for 10 minutes, drain, and then puree the chilies in a blender with the garlic, onion, thyme, oregano, peppercorns, salt, bay leaves, vinegar, and orange juice. Add a little water to the blender if necessary to form a thick, smooth paste.

Rub the pork thoroughly with all of the marinade and refrigerate overnight.

Place the marinated pork with the avocado leaves and bay leaves inside a Crock-Pot, add half a bottle of your favorite Mexican beer (or if you live in Williamsburg, Brooklyn, Pabst Blue Ribbon, known as PBR locally), and cook for 10 hours on low. The meat will be falling off the bone, and indescribably delicious.

Spicy Guacamole

I have made many a guacamole in my life. This is the easiest and closest to a traditional that I have found. Luis and I like it very spicy so we use about ten serrano peppers with the seeds. I went to a restaurant called Rayuela in New York that added shrimp and crabmeat—it was delicious! So don't get nervous—just play around and have fun.

2 plum tomatoes, seeded and diced

1 medium white onion, finely diced

5 to 10 serrano or jalapeño peppers, seeded or not, finely diced

1 bunch cilantro, rinsed and finely chopped

4 ripe Hass avocados

2 ripe limes

Salt and pepper

Dice your tomatoes, onion, and chilies and chop your cilantro. Combine these in a large bowl.

Cut your avocados in half. Remove the pit by putting your knife lengthwise across the middle of the pit; gently pull the pit out and discard. Take the avocado meat out of the skins and add it to the bowl with your other ingredients.

Cut your limes in half and squeeze the juice into your mix. I take a potato masher at this point and mash the whole mixture up until smooth. Add salt and pepper to taste. It will take much more salt than one thinks. Taste, and then serve. Don't worry about the calories—you only live once!

CHAPTER ELEVEN

Bright Lights, Dark Passages

And those who were seen dancing were thought to be
insane by those who could not hear the music.
—FRIEDRICH NIETZSCHE

During the week in June that my father and I spent together in Santa Fe shortly after my mother's death, while I was out there teaching for the Moving People Dance, we came up with what we thought was the brilliant idea of hosting a full-blown family reunion at the Eagle Nest house later that summer. The house wouldn't be finished, but we figured everyone could bring tents and sleeping bags. We would bring Mom's ashes and lots of food and have a party in her honor. I invited all of Mom's family, and several other friends—Pop and I were both excited. Almost immediately, however, the terrible alchemy of family gatherings began to boil and bubble. Mom's Navajo sisters started calling to say they were very upset that Mom's ashes had not yet been put in the ground—they said it was causing havoc of all kinds, and they didn't think they could attend the reunion. By the time August rolled around, my excitement about bringing all of my family together had been transmuted to dread.

The day for our August adventure finally came and Luis and I headed out to New Mexico, where Pop picked us up at the Albuquerque airport and drove us over the mountains in his RV to Eagle Nest. Pop had positioned a framed photograph of Mom against the windshield of the RV in a way that projected a magnified reflection of her face back at any passengers, and she was smiling out at me as we bumped our way through the twisting mountain roads. It was a little eerie. I sat in the big swiveling easy chair next to the driver's seat, where Mom always used to sit, and at one point Pop turned to me and told me it made him feel powerful to have me sitting there. Also eerie. Just as we were approaching Eagle Nest he announced that he had a special surprise for us—he had invited a few people from the community to meet me and have dinner with us the following night.

"That's nice," I said. "How many?"

"Oh, I don't know," Pop answered. "I put an announcement in the local paper: 'Meet and Greet at a Dinner with Jock Soto, New York City Ballet Dancer and New Resident of Eagle Nest.' Somewhere between fifty and a hundred? We'll see."

Luis and I looked at each other in disbelief. We hoped he was joking—but he was not.

The next day Luis and I got up early and shopped at the tiny Valley grocery and cooked like demons all day—grilled sausage with cannellini beans, penne Bolognese, tomato-and-mozzarella salad. Everything was ready just in time as the first guests began arriving promptly at five. About sixty people showed up in the end—everyone was very nice, and my father was especially proud that the mayor of Eagle Nest, a woman, attended. After dinner, as it began to get dark, someone hung a bedsheet over the fireplace and set up chairs and showed *Water Flowing Together.* I hadn't realized this would be part of the evening, and Luis and I chose instead to sit outside and admire the silence of the mountains and the amazing star-studded western sky I remembered so well from my youth. Our half-built house looked huge silhouetted against the night sky and the glistening lake beyond, and it already looked friendly and familiar too, as if it were waiting patiently for us to come back to it. Was it possible that after all these years in New York I might be able to make a home out west? The concept seemed wild.

A few days later the official "family reunion" weekend launched and various guests began funneling into the tiny mountain town—Kiko and his wife, Deb; Deb's aunt Carol and cousin Rick; Pop's friends Stu and Donna; my Navajo filmmaker friend Nanobah Becker; my nephew Trevor; Kiko's friends Kent and Lisa; my aunt Shelley and uncle Kevin and their son Andrew; my cousin Dawn and her partner, Jeannie; my former SAB classmate Jefferson Baum, who works nearby at the school of the Aspen Santa Fe Ballet, and his girlfriend, Carla.

Mom's youngest sister, Shelley, was the only sibling who made it to Eagle Nest for the reunion, in the end. (Shelley is the baby of the family—twenty years younger than Mom—and the only one of Mom's siblings who also broke with tradition and married someone outside the tribe, my big, white-skinned, redheaded uncle Kevin.) We were a motley but happy

crew, bound by either blood or friendship or both, as we gathered in the midst of a torrential downpour at the Lucky Shoe
Saloon for our "reunion" celebration luncheon. It was not a
particularly formal affair—we were surrounded by more television screens than I could count broadcasting every imagin-
able sports event, and conversations had to be fit between several highly competitive pool games (Kiko and Deb are both
league players). Most of my mother's siblings were conspicu-
ously absent, but for a few brief hours on a rainy afternoon, a
respectable chunk of my extended "family" gathered to spend
time together and celebrate one another. We ate, we drank,
we toasted Kiko's and Kevin's birthdays. We toasted our beloved Mama Jo. We hugged, we laughed, we reminisced. We
plotted, vaguely, for more gatherings in the future. And then,
as the sun finally drove away the storm clouds and reminded
us that there was still a bright day waiting out there, Luis and
I paid the bill and we all left. I had survived my first stint hosting a "family reunion."

When I got back to New York I was exhausted, and I
was overcome by the same feelings that I used to get on
the few occasions when I visited my family out west during
my years with the NYCB: shock (tinged with guilt) at the
differences between the worlds my biological family and
I inhabited, and sadness at how little we knew about one
another's lives. My feelings during the very rare occasions
when my parents actually made it to New York to visit me
were always just as confusing. I remember Mom and Pop
coming to visit Ulrik and me once when we were living in
an apartment on Twentieth Street. We had to move a television into the living room for my father, who even then had a

hard-core addiction to the small screen. Pop sat there, glued to the TV all day, and at one point, without diverting his gaze from whatever he was watching, I remember he said, "Get me a drink, would you, Eric?"

"His name is Ulrik, and you'll get your own damn drink" was my rude response. Not attractive, but I was wrestling with all kinds of anger and suppressed emotions at the time, in large part because of my father's continued open and intense disapproval of homosexuals. Here they were, staying with me and my live-in boyfriend, and I *still* had not officially addressed the issue of my homosexuality with my parents. As it turned out, I would not find the courage to approach the topic until I was thirty, at which point my mother howled with laughter at my delusion that I could be "breaking any news." But for years and years, my father's implied dissatisfaction with me and my own failure to be honest made visits with my parents incredibly unpleasant and tense. I think some part of me also must have been afraid that if I wasn't careful, the life I had worked so hard to leave behind would come crawling out of my parents' bodies as they sat there in my living room, passively watching TV, sneak up, and steal me back again.

With my promotion to principal dancer in 1985, the world I was living in became even more dramatically different from the world I had been born in. I began dancing more and more lead parts with Heather, but also with a dizzying array of other amazingly talented ballerinas—Maria Calegari, Judith Fugate, Patricia McBride, Darci Kistler, Stephanie Saland, Lourdes Lopez, Diana White, Kyra Nichols, and many others. In my late-night postperformance escapades I was spending all my offstage time with a glamorous new surrogate family that included Heather and Peter, Peter's son, Nilas, (also a NYCB dancer), Ulrik, and a few other dancers—most notably John Bass, Peter Boal, and Bruce Padgett—who were our closest friends. I remember hearing a rumor that some of the other dancers in the company referred to this inner circle as the "Royal Family" and feeling a twinge of discomfort. Somewhere inside me I sensed that there was something innately inappropriate about *my* being a member of an exclusive clique. But the situation was extremely seductive, and I pushed any misgivings away.

At night I moved with my new family from center stage at Lincoln Center to center stage at the Manhattan clubs that were all the rage in the mideighties—Nell's on Fourteenth Street, the Pyramid Club on Avenue A, the Boy Bar, Palladium, the World, Wah Wah Hut, and, of course, the Odeon and Indochine, both run by Keith McNally, and the Canal Bar, run by Keith's brother, Brian McNally. I remember at one point we were all given little keys that read NELL'S to attach to our key chains, which allowed us to cut all the lines and get into the clubs for free. We felt like hotshots—we were becoming *somebodies*.

Everyone in our little group—especially Heather, it seemed to me—was suddenly gathering more and more attention from the world at large. One night the screen actress Jodie Foster was sitting at a nearby table at the Canal Bar, and she stared and stared and stared at Heather. Another night at Il Cantinore in the Village we met the writer Tama Janowitz and the exotic Paige Powell, close friend and assistant to the famous pop art icon Andy Warhol, both of whom later introduced us to Warhol himself. I'll never forget the

first time I was invited to join Andy for dinner at the Algon-
quin Hotel. When I asked if I could bring some friends, he
said, "Yeah, great. That's great." I took ten friends in the end,
unabashed little upstart that I was, including Heather, with
whom Andy instantly became obsessed. He then began attending every ballet, always sitting in the same spot up front
(Balanchine's former seats, in the first ring, which we had
provided), his white head luminescent in the dark theater as
he stared intently at the stage throughout the performances.
After the performances we would head downtown to meet
Warhol and various members of his eclectic entourage—
painter Francesco Clemente and his wife, Alba; the jeweler
John Reinhold; singer Debbie Harry; artists Alex Katz, Ste-
phen Sprouse, Keith Haring, and Jean-Michel Basquiat—
wherever they had gathered. Often it was at a huge group
table at Indochine, and when we arrived, Andy—who could
be the most peculiar mix of quiet, fascinating, nasty, and flir-
tatious all at once—would murmur, "So great you came. You
guys were great tonight." We would drink and eat and dance
and carry on all night—I never knew who paid.

One day Andy called and said he wanted to take photographs and paint portraits of Heather, Ulrik, and me as
Christmas presents for us, so we headed over to The Factory
for our photo session. Afterward we went to Mr. Chow's,
another regular haunt where Andy liked to hold court in a
favorite corner. Keith and Jean-Michel would set up a boom
box nearby and disappear in a cloud of marijuana smoke. Everyone I met seemed to be both talented and strange, and life
itself was so fast and wild and exciting—surely we were all
hot on the trail of at least fifteen minutes of fame.

On several occasions in those years Peter, Heather, Ulrik, and I were invited to dinner at Lincoln Kirstein's house, as ballet *objets* to spice up parties when Kirstein was entertaining potential donors to the NYCB. Among the regular guests was a wealthy woman named Frances Schreuder, who had been hugely generous to the ballet community, but who ran into a sticky patch when it was alleged that she had urged her son to kill her father (her son's grandfather) so that she could inherit his money. All of this seemed scandalous in an entertaining, wacky art-world way; and then there was the titillating mystery of Lincoln Kirstein's wife—a woman named Fidelma who seemed never to be a part of our gatherings. After the dinners we would turn to one another as we hit the streets to head off to whatever after-parties there were on that night and ask, "Where in the world was Fidelma?"

On the surface, our lives may have seemed to be hip and glittering and glamorous, but during these same years a tinge of darkness—of recklessness and mishap and even of death—was also seeping in at the edges, staining the studied beauty of our ballet endeavors and the roaring gaiety of our nightlife. Balanchine's illness, followed by his death in 1983, had been the first dark shadow cast over our beautiful playground. As the seasons unfolded, the tragedies multiplied. In September 1985, just months after I had been promoted to principal, the whole company was badly shaken when our beloved John Bass—a talented corps dancer and a man of high spirits and incredible wit—got mysteriously ill. John had come to a dinner at the Gruens' one night with his right eye stuck shut—he didn't know why this was happening, but he said he was going to the doctor the next day. The next thing we knew John had been diagnosed with a rare cancer, and quarantined in the hospital—and then he died. It was awful. No one understood exactly what had happened, but the doctors and newspapers all said that he had died of lymphatic cancer. We would learn soon enough that he had died of something else, a dreadful new disease everyone was calling "the gay disease": it was AIDS, and John was only twenty-nine when he died. All of us who knew John were deeply saddened and confused by his death, and as the deadly statistics about AIDS began to unfold, and rumors began to spread about the many ways it could be contracted, the situation became terrifying. A killer had been unleashed in our midst—a silent, unpredictable killer.

Not five months after John's death, in February 1986, another tragedy rocked the company. Joseph Duell, a beautiful dancer and promising young choreographer with the company, leaped from his fifth-floor apartment and died. Joseph had been promoted to principal less than two years earlier, and he was emerging as a major talent. Just the day before his death I had watched him give a disturbing, strangely distant performance of the first movement of *Symphony in C*. Everyone knew that Joseph was deeply committed to his art, but that he had struggled in the past with depression and other demons. But his death was unthinkable. Like John, Joseph was only twenty-nine. How could someone so young and strong and full of light be conquered by darkness? As one of our fellow dancers, Toni Bentley, wrote at the time in a piece about Joseph for the *New York Times*: "The source of a dancer's power is the energy that distinguishes life from death. For suicide to enter such a world as ours totally dislocates us, our values and our visions."

The unforgiving nature of a performance schedule can be a godsend in times of extreme stress and sorrow—whatever else happens, life and art must continue to play out from moment to moment for a dancer onstage. The company had danced the day Balanchine died and we had danced the day John Bass died and we danced the day Joseph Duell died. On all of these occasions we danced for and in honor of our absent brethren, carrying our confusion and sadness with us through our airy leaps and turns, letting whatever feelings were trapped inside us give color to our expression in that moment—this was the only way we knew how to process life. This was what I had been trained to do for years. You don't talk about it, you don't analyze it, you don't dissect it—you go to class or you go to rehearsal or you go to the theater and you just dance.

When my twenty-first birthday rolled around that April, Ulrik threw a huge party for me at Brian McNally's trendy Canal Bar. It was a strange and surreal experience for me to be the "guest of honor" at a gathering that was packed with famous New York artists and dancers and "celebrities" of all types. In addition to the ballet crowd and Andy Warhol and his superhip entourage, a smattering of high-profile people like Ray Charles, the Reverend Jesse Jackson, and Fran Lebowitz all came to celebrate with me. Ulrik documented the event with a photo album that had captions under the pictures, and I will never forget the shot of me standing on a table, screaming something at the top of my lungs. Beneath it he posted the caption: "At age 21 Jock finally DOES have a voice!"

It was true. Maybe my promotion to principal dancer and my arrival at the milestone of legal adulthood had given me more confidence and a clearer sense of who I was. But for whatever reason, for the first time I was beginning to think—and sometimes even to speak—for myself. Although I'm sure dancing so many new roles onstage had boosted my confidence in general, in retrospect it seems obvious that an important factor behind my growing sense of self, in addition to the passage of time, was my increasingly intense relationship with Heather, on- and offstage. As Heather and I became more established as partners onstage, and more attuned to the specific nuances of each other's style, I could allow myself to explore and experiment more. It was always an exciting and often a quite daring experience to perform with Heather, because she could be counted on to challenge me while we were out there. She might take off for a turn when I was still ten feet away, or add extra pirouettes as if to say, "Ha, take that!" I learned to counter with challenges of my own. In the *Nutcracker*, in the grand pas de deux in the second act, I remember trying to do every turn or arabesque with one hand instead of two. It was exhilarating to dance such beautiful and complicated ballets with this sleek, spiky, edgy ballerina whom Balanchine had called his "wild orchid." For all the boldness and complexity of her movements, Heather never made a sound with her pointe shoes, and audiences were transformed by the purity with which her dancing married the music. I could understand why someone like Andy Warhol had become fascinated with her; many people were. Heather's bright blue eyes alone, with their long, lush eyelashes, were mesmerizing. When Andy did our portraits, he did several of Heather's eyes alone.

Those intense eyes of Heather's, and the way they could lock in on you—it comes back to me every time I recall the dark February day in 1987 when another sudden tragedy rocked our world. It was a cold and rainy afternoon—in the windowless New York State Theater you could never see or smell the rain, but sometimes you could hear the rumblings of thunder exploding outside—and Heather and I were about to dance in a matinee performance of Peter Martins's *L'Histoire du Soldat*. I was just about to make my entrance when a stage manager came up to me. "I hear your friend died today," he said. I looked at him, confused. "What are you talking about?" I asked. "I have to go onstage." "Your friend, the guy with the white wig," he answered.

That was how I learned that Andy Warhol had died. It was so confusing, but I had to make my entrance. I didn't have time to react, so I just walked onstage and began the pas de deux. I knew Heather could feel something was wrong. She kept sending me fierce looks with those piercing blue eyes of hers, seeking mine at every opportunity. We finished dancing, and the moment we were offstage I told her the news. I remember feeling shocked, and also scared and angry. When someone backstage reported that Andy had died in the hospital after a gallbladder operation, I refused to believe it at first. How was this possible? Something awful was happening in the world. I was twenty-one years old and my friends were dying.

Andy's death that February was one of many profound moments that Heather and I would share, in life and on and off the stage, during the fifteen years we danced together. The combination of these intense experiences and the sheer

LEFT: Papa Joe with Baby Jock (left) and Kiko (in hat) at the Goldfield Ghost Town in Apache Junction, Arizona. Picture taken by Mama Jo. *(Courtesy of Josephine Towne Soto)*

ABOVE: Mama Jo in full regalia, ready to perform the traditional Navajo hoop dance at a powwow. Mama Jo made her costume, and her father, Grandpa Bud, made the hoops. *(Courtesy of the Soto family)*

LEFT: Executing a passé as a student at the Phoenix School of Ballet. *(Courtesy of Josephine Towne Soto)*

BELOW: Performing with a fellow student at the Phoenix School of Ballet in the annual Christmas show. *(Courtesy of the Soto family)*

RIGHT: With Papa Joe and Mama Jo on one of our rodeo tours. *(Courtesy of the Soto family)*

BELOW: Papa Joe, definitely an "outsider" on the reservation. *(Courtesy of the Soto family)*

ABOVE: Papa Joe, Mama Jo, me, and Kiko (standing) in our famous *Partridge Family*–style portrait, taken at the local strip mall. I wore that vest for the next ten years. *(Courtesy of the Soto family)*

LEFT: At age twelve, dancing the Spanish section of Yvonne Mounsey's version of *The Nutcracker* at the Westside School of Ballet in Santa Monica, California. *(Courtesy of the Soto family)*

School of American Ballet teacher Stanley Williams, choreographer and artistic director of New York City Ballet George Balanchine, Dagoberto Nieves, and me, during rehearsal of August Bournonville's *Jockey Dance* for my first workshop as a student at SAB. (© *Martha Swope*)

ABOVE: Rehearsing *The Magic Flute* with Peter Martins and Katrina Killian for my second workshop at SAB in 1981. (© *Steven Caras*)

LEFT: Performing the "Gigue" solo in Balanchine's *Mozartiana* during my first year with the company. (© *Steven Caras*)

RIGHT: Dancing the role of Luke in the new company production of *The Magic Flute* in 1982. *(© Steven Caras)*

BELOW: My debut in Mr. B's *Symphony in Three Movements*, dancing the second movement pas de deux with Maria Calegari. *(© 1983 Martha Swope)*

ABOVE: Dancing with Heather Watts in *Concerto for Two Solo Pianos*, the first ballet that Peter Martins choreographed on the two of us. *(© Martha Swope)*

LEFT: At a black-tie event in Paris, with Ulrik (center) and colleague John Bass, on my first European tour with the company in 1983.

LEFT: A big thrill for me came when I danced the "Rubies" section of Balanchine's *Jewels*—the very ballet that had inspired me at age four—with Heather Watts. (© *1983 Martha Swope*)

BELOW: Dancing the "Royal Navy" section of Balanchine's *Union Jack* in 1986. Almost twenty years later, I would dance the same role in my retirement performance. (© *Steven Caras*)

LEFT: Whooping it up with the inimitable Lourdes Lopez in the first movement of Balanchine's *Western Symphony*. (© *1984 Martha Swope*)

RIGHT: With Ray Charles, Heather Watts, and Peter Martins at the premiere of Martins's *A Fool for You* at the American Music Festival in 1988. (© *Paul Kolnik*)

RIGHT: Performing Jerome Robbins's *Afternoon of a Faun* with the sublime Darci Kistler. (© *Paul Kolnik*)

BELOW: Heather and me in the second movement of Balanchine's *Bugaku*—one of the ballets we would perform together at her retirement. (© *Steven Caras*)

ABOVE: An emotional end to a long partnership came when Heather retired in 1995. (© *Steven Caras*)

LEFT: Back to my Native roots—sort of—afloat in a canoe on a lake in the Adirondacks with one of Bruce Weber's handsome pups. (*Courtesy of Bruce Weber*)

Playing Bernardo in the fight scene of Jerome Robbins's *West Side Story Suite*. *(© Paul Kolnik)*

When Christopher Wheeldon choreographed *Polyphonia* on Wendy Whelan and me, it was the beginning of an exciting new collaboration for all of us. *(© Paul Kolnik)*

Miranda Weese and I dance the second movement of *Mercurial Manoeuvres*, choreographed on us by Christopher Wheeldon. *(© Paul Kolnik)*

After the Rain was the last ballet Christopher Wheeldon choreographed on Wendy and me, about six months before I retired. *(© Paul Kolnik)*

Me and Luis, the year we met.
(Courtesy of the author)

BELOW: Teaching a pas de deux class at SAB—one of my favorite classes. *(© Ellen Crane)*

Bowing at my retirement performance, June 2005. *(© Johanna Weber)*

volume of time we logged together seemed to bring us closer and closer with each passing month—in retrospect, it seems probable that I was relating to her more and more as a kind of surrogate mother. We went everywhere together and did everything together. I admired and trusted her, and asked for her advice about everything. In fact, there is no doubt in my mind that it was both Peter's and Heather's mentorship and support in those tender years of my late teens and early twenties that gave me the courage to try to formulate an identity of my own. I started looking around and thinking for myself, and after a while I began to consider new options in my private life as well as onstage.

Ulrik had noticed my newfound confidence enough to acknowledge it in his photo caption that read, "Jock finally DOES have a voice," but I think I shocked both of us when I proved my new independence by starting an affair with another man. I'd like to blame my actions on the Pyramid Bar and the disco night that they used to host there every week— but I think it had a lot more to do with youth and lust and good old-fashioned paybacks. Ulrik's dalliances were really wearing on me. The first night that I noticed John Beal at the Pyramid's Sunday disco event it was because he was noticing me, staring holes into me from somewhere to my right as I ordered drinks at the bar. When I turned to look I was astounded—I didn't think it was possible for anyone to be as good-looking as Ulrik. We said hello, and exchanged names. When he intercepted me on the way to the men's room a little later, I explained that I had a boyfriend—a boyfriend who was, in fact, right across the room from us.

When I went back to the Pyramid Bar the following

Sunday, John was there again. This time when we talked, briefly, we also exchanged numbers. I was slightly horrified by this brazen act, but when he called and invited me to lunch a few days later, I accepted. We ate at the Tomato Café in Chelsea—I will never forget it—and I was so aware that I was doing something bad that I couldn't touch my food. John positioned his knees outside mine under the table, and kept pushing my knees together with his, until I had to ask him to stop. I was upset by this rendezvous, but when I went to the Pyramid Bar on the following Sunday, I was armed and in a premeditated mood for crime, whether or not I knew it at the time. I was on a cassette-making jag in those days, and I often made tapes of different songs built around some special theme. Before leaving for the Pyramid that night, I loaded a copy of my most recent cassette of assorted love songs—"Don't Make Me Over," "I Say a Little Prayer," "Tainted Love," and other classics—into my pocket. It just seemed like a good idea to me as I left the house, and I couldn't say exactly why.

When Ulrik and Heather got into a big argument about something later that night—I can't remember what; they were both such aggressive and intelligent verbal wizards, conversation was often a blood sport for them—I looked at Peter Martins's son, Nilas, and gave him the "Let's get outta here" look. Needless to say, when Nilas and I left I came up with the bright idea to call John—from a pay phone in the street (because this was still the pre–cell phone era)—and we wound up heading down to John's apartment in the East Village (parts of which were actually kind of scary in the eighties) so that I could deliver my cassette as a gift. The rest is not really what you would call history, but it is my history. John and I started dating, and before too long I moved (along with the two beautiful shar-peis, named Lily and Sam, whom Ulrik and I owned together) to a place of my own—a whole two blocks away from the apartment Ulrik and I had shared. John and I hung out for about a year. He was a lovely man, an excellent cook, and also a dancer with several modern dance troupes—including the Trockadero ballet, no less. I was shocked when I learned about the latter. He was extremely ugly en pointe in a tutu, but he was gorgeous offstage.

When you are dancing ten or more hours a day, pouring everything you have into rehearsals and performances, it is difficult to concentrate intelligently on much of anything else. It's no secret that dancers' private lives, which get wedged into the narrow slot of time that is left after they tend to their first love, can get notoriously strange and convoluted—and mine was no exception. Recently I was flipping through a "Week-at-a-Glance" diary from 1988 that I kept when I was living on my own for the first time—one of a couple of failed diary attempts on my part during this period. I was reminded of how jam-packed my life had been in those days—both professionally and personally. In the month of January I mention fifteen different ballets I was performing or rehearsing, including *The Nutcracker, Allegro Brilliante, Piano Pieces, Afternoon of a Faun, Agon, Brahms/Handel, Liebeslieder Walzer, Symphony in C, Ecstatic Orange, Vienna Waltzes, Stravinsky Violin Concerto, Jewels,* and *Bugaku.* Sometimes I was performing two or even three of these ballets in a single day. And of course the visits to bars and restaurants in the same one-month period outnumber the ballets by a factor of at least three to one. The notation "got very drunk," scrawled across the page as a kind of explanation for why nothing else is written there, appears with embarrassing regularity. January 17 offers a typical entry:

> Sunday. Pop's birthday. Must call. He turns half a century today.
>   Danced Liebeslieder and Brahms-Handel.
>   Called Pop, he was very into making me feel sorry for him. He asked what I sent him, I said nothing. He said I should think of him more often, and not hate him. Dinner at Peter Wolff's. Got very very drunk. Everybody fought.
>   To Indochine, then to Pyramid for "the one last nightcap." Then home.

A number of significant milestones also occurred within this one year. In February my grandma Rachel died and I flew home to the reservation. ("It was very sad, lots of crying. Went to bed thinking: I *must* get home to New York, how will I get home to New York tomorrow?" I wrote in my Week-at-a-Glance.) I flew to Virgin Gorda (in the British Virgin Islands) with Heather for a week of vacation. That spring in the company's American Music Festival (which introduced a total of twenty-two ballets and eighteen choreographers) I danced in five new ballets—Jean-Pierre Bonnefoux's *Five*, Robert Weiss's *Archetypes*, Laura Dean's *Space*, and Peter Martins's *Black and White* and *A Fool for You* with Ray Charles—as well as in the company premiere of Richard Tanner's *Sonatas and Interludes*. In June, Heather and I spent a week of vacation in Connecticut at Peter's country house ("Eating Drinking Relaxing" is scrawled across every diary page for seven days). In July I went with the company to Saratoga; in August we went on tour to Greece, Italy, France, and Japan. In between all of this I got my learner's permit to drive (finally!), worked with Heather at God's Love We Deliver to raise several thousand dollars for AIDS relief, did several interviews and photo shoots for various publications, and celebrated Ulrik's retirement from the company. Somewhere in here I suppose I must have walked poor Lily and Sam.

What with my dancing and my drinking and my running all over New York and the world at large, it's no wonder I couldn't find the time or emotional resources to establish a successful stable relationship with John—or anyone, to be honest. To compound matters, throughout this period, when I was supposedly establishing my independence by living on my own and seeing my new boyfriend, my Week-at-a-Glance reminds me that I was also having frequent dinners and rendezvous—and many very long late-night arguments over the telephone—with Ulrik. At some point in here John moved to Paris for a while to pursue a modeling career, leaving me essentially alone again. Sometimes—especially when we are young and hotheaded—it is our more destructive relationships that are the most compelling, and the path of most resistance is the one we prefer to follow. For whatever reason, after a year of living "alone," I allowed the very articulate, complicated, handsome, and persuasive Ulrik to convince me to come back and live with him again. As a friend of mine likes to say, sometimes a mistake worth making once seems worth making twice.

It was pretty clear immediately after we got back together that things were not going well. When Ulrik left the NYCB he had gone into the restaurant business, and as the weeks passed our relationship went from disjointed to disconnected. For several months neither one of us seemed to have the free time—or any overlapping breaks in our schedules, or, for that matter, the emotional skills—to try to address the issue. We just let things unravel and coexisted with Lily and Sam in the big duplex apartment we had rented. Finally the day came when I had to admit to myself that I couldn't go on. Over the course of a few weeks I packed all my belongings—Ulrik was so busy I'm not sure he even noticed the boxes piling up—and when I found a place (yes, two blocks away again) I called movers and Lily, Sam, and I moved out. I was twenty-five years old, and I was finally—really and truly this time, I told myself—ready to try to grow up and live life on my own.

Chop till You Drop: A Last-minute Meal for Fifty or More

WHEN MY FATHER first dropped the bomb that he had published an announcement in the local newspaper for a "meet and greet" dinner at our house the day after we arrived in Eagle Nest, Luis and I looked at each other and wondered if we should just turn around and get on a plane back to New York. I am proud to report, however, that we pulled it off. We proved that—even in a tiny mountain town with limited grocery resources and cooking in a strange and only semi-equipped kitchen—it is actually possible to get up early in the morning and shop for and prepare a full meal for more than fifty guests by 5 p.m. the same day.

Our menu took shape as we shopped, according to what was available at the Valley Market in the nearby town of Angel Fire: grilled sausages with cannellini beans, green salad, tomato-and-mozzarella salad, garlic bread, and—as the foundation for our megafeast—the ever-expandable, crowd-pleasing penne with Bolognese sauce. The recipe that follows serves eight, but just multiply by ten if you have to feed a village on short notice.

My Penne Polonaise

SERVES 8

When I began making this recipe as a young ballet dancer I could never remember the name Bolognese, so I started calling it Penne Polonaise, in honor of a familiar ballet step. Over the years, the name stuck. I learned a little trick from our friend Chef Cesare Casella. When the sauce is almost finished add a sprinkle or two of an Indian spice called garam masala. It marries everything and brings a special flavor to the sauce.

2 carrots, peeled and
  roughly chopped
3 celery stalks, roughly
  chopped
1 large onion, roughly
  chopped
10 cloves peeled garlic
  (or less if you're a wimp)
Salt
1 box of penne pasta
2½ pounds mixed ground
  veal, pork, and beef
2 to 3 tablespoons olive oil

1 28-ounce can plum
  tomatoes (reserve the
  liquid)
Pepper
1 tablespoon each finely
  chopped fresh thyme,
  oregano, and rosemary
1 teaspoon garam masala
  (available at gourmet
  and Indian markets)
½ to 1 cup grated
  Parmesan cheese

Get out your faithful Cuisinart and process the carrots, celery, onion, and garlic in batches to make something similar to a rough cornmeal. Set aside.

Put a large pot of water, generously salted, on to boil for the pasta.

In a separate large pot brown the meat in 2 tablespoons of olive oil. When the meat is thoroughly browned, add your vegetable mixture and cook on medium heat for another 5 minutes, stirring regularly.

Empty the tomatoes and their liquid into a bowl and break up the tomatoes by squeezing them gently (another lesson from my mother, who insisted that food should always be handled with respect) and add to the meat. Season with salt and pepper to taste and add your herbs. Bring to a boil; then turn the heat down to low, cover the sauce, and cook for about 20 minutes, stirring every now and then, so it doesn't stick to the bottom of the pan. Add the garam masala and cook for another 10 minutes.

Meanwhile, cook the penne in boiling water for 2 minutes less than the recommended time, so it's al dente, and then use a slotted spoon to transfer the pasta to the sauce.

Add ½ cup of grated Parmesan to your sauce and stir. If the sauce seems too thick or gummy, you can add ½ cup or so of the pasta water and the remaining olive oil. (I love a lot of cheese, so the pasta water is always necessary.) Taste, and adjust the seasoning.

Serve with more grated cheese, Italian bread, and a very good red wine. Whatever you do, don't launch into a Polonaise while carrying this to the table, or you will be wearing your dinner.

CHAPTER TWELVE

Exploring New Country

*Astaire was not a sexual animal, but he made his
partners look so extraordinarily related to him.*

—MIKHAIL BARYSHNIKOV

Ballet is Woman" is one of Balanchine's most frequently
quoted statements about his art, and to project woman
in her most transcendent and absolute form you must have
man. This was the ideal of ballet that I was working so hard
to achieve every time I stepped onstage, particularly with my
partnering roles. When I first started to partner as a teenager,
I had been understandably nervous—not only was I a mere
upstart dancing with famous ballerinas, I was also completely
inexperienced when it came to passion and romance—and I
was gay. Would I be able to project a classic male presence
convincingly? Could I interact with a woman onstage in a
way that would bring the transcendent beauty of the love
story alive, as I had seen so many of my idols do? But the
wonderful thing about dance is that in the end it really is all
about movement and *action*, and I could worry about these

things for only so long before it was time to just get out there and try. I learned early on that if I cast off my anxieties and turned to my partner with openness and trust, the music and the choreography would lift us into the character and emotion and movement of our roles. The key for me, to cite another Balanchine quote, seemed to be "Don't think, just do."

I quickly discovered that I was quite comfortable partnering—I liked the less-exposed position behind a woman and I seemed to have an instinctive sense for where a ballerina needed to be and how to get her there. I liked making myself as quiet and invisible as possible behind my ballerinas. I worked specifically on ways to keep my hands hidden, how to give subtle support so that my ballerinas could appear to take off and float, landing effortlessly and silently, like the sublime creatures they were. Most important, I learned that there was never any need to fake the emotion of a ballet. All the romance and feeling will come barreling through you, as real as the floorboards beneath your feet, if you dance full out.

By the time I was twenty-five I had proved myself as a competent and even skilled ballet partner with many ballerinas. But when I danced with Heather something bigger was happening; I could feel the two of us entering a more profound realm of collaboration, especially in certain ballets we worked on with Peter—such as *Songs of the Auvergne*, *Ecstatic Orange*, *Fearful Symmetries*. In all of these the three of us were exploring exciting new combinations of lyrical and edgy dancing within a single piece, and experimenting with the ways our bodies could be manipulated to express emotion. Choreographers often get visions and ideas in subliminal ways—there has been speculation that Balanchine's brilliant use of the deliberate manipulation of his dancer's bodies in ballets like *Agon* and *Episodes* may have been a subliminal reflection of the physical demands of his life with his wife at the time, Tanaquil Le Clercq, a beautiful ballerina who was tragically paralyzed by polio in her prime. I know Peter was hugely influenced and inspired by many aspects of Balanchine's choreography, but I think he also began to mine a new source of creativity by exploring the specific physical possibilities that arose minute by minute, hour by hour, when he and Heather and I shut ourselves in a studio with some music. It was really exciting. Heather and I had become established as a well-known onstage couple, one the audience both anticipated and enjoyed, and as our repertory expanded, our bodies seemed to fit together more and more naturally, as if specifically designed to be twisted and intertwined in strange and new ways.

The increased intensity and creativity Heather and I felt onstage was echoed in—and perhaps facilitated by—parallel changes in our private lives. Because I was single for the first time in ten years, I had more free time to spend with Heather offstage. As it happened, Heather also had more time to spend with me. Heather and Peter's already stormy relationship had been upgraded to a high monsoon category by the late eighties; the two of them were constantly breaking up and then getting back together, only to break up again. I found these romantic upsets very disturbing, probably because I was craving stability and Peter and Heather were basically my surrogate parents. In fact, I wanted them to get married and solidify our little family so badly that I would sometimes fantasize about and plan their imaginary wedding. I may have been a little slow to grasp the reality of the situation, but time would make things clear soon enough when Heather and Peter broke up for good and each fell in love with someone else—in both cases, as it turned out, with the person whom they would eventually marry. Heather's new love was a dashing young dancer named Damian Woetzel, who had joined the company in 1985; Peter's was our beautiful and well-established star ballerina Darci Kistler.

All the relationships in my private life seemed to be shifting during this period, and because my private and professional lives were completely entangled, just navigating life on a day-to-day basis could get pretty tricky. Heather and Peter were both still close to Ulrik; Peter was still choreographing new ballets on Heather and me; and I was partnering both Heather and Darci. I told myself that predicaments of this kind must arise in every profession, not just in the intense and inbred world of a ballet company, and I tried to simplify the challenges of juggling all the personality clashes by reminding myself that at the end of each day I knew exactly where my loyalties would lie: with the company and the integrity of our work. I knew it was not the first time nasty private conflicts had threatened to disrupt the professional responsibilities of company dancers—this happens all the time—and I knew the standard operating procedure for such situations. All grudges and differences of opinion and personal problems had to be laid down outside the studio door, so that whatever work went on inside the studio or on the stage could be conducted with a purity of effort and intent. That was the way it had to be, and that was what everyone tried to do.

Peter was on his usual prolific tear at the time, instituting all kinds of innovative programs and initiatives for the company and constantly choreographing new ballets. He had me working with him on a sequence of very different ballets—*Fearful Symmetries* (with Heather and Merrill Ashley), *Delight of the Muses* (with Darci), *Jazz: Six Syncopated Movements* (with Heather), and *Sinfonia* (with Darci and Wendy Whelan and Yvonne Borree)—and I felt that in our choreographing sessions we were communicating better than ever. During this period, when I was working so intensely with Peter and ping-ponging as a partner between Heather and Darci, the NYCB choreographer Richard Tanner also tapped me to work with him on two beautiful new ballets—*Ancient Airs and Dances* and *A Schubert Sonata*. Dick is very smart and very musical, and his choreography is quite intricate and fast. Working with him on a pas de deux with Heather was especially exciting because, although he was very involved and demanding, Dick left a lot open to us dancers. As if all of these challenges weren't enough, another amazing opportunity—and one of the greatest honors of my career—came my way during this same time period when choreographer Lynne Taylor-Corbett began working on her ballet *Chiaroscuro* with me and several other dancers. I was completely oblivious to the special tribute Lynne was paying me as we began working; all I knew was that I was constantly onstage and working with a series of dancers who came and joined me in a fascinating and demanding ballet. I really loved it. It wasn't until after the premiere that I understood that Lynne had envisioned the ballet specifically as a tribute to and a showcase for me. I was stunned. We had never really talked about it, but somehow she had intuited essential qualities of my Native American heritage—an earthiness and spirituality, and the intricate relationships within a large clan—that I'm not sure I was even aware of myself.

Learning all of these new ballets one after another in such an insanely busy whirl was demanding, but I was growing more confident about my own creativity, both as a dancer and as a collaborator in the exciting process of choreography. I could feel my skills maturing into a fluent, almost patented language that allowed my fellow dancers and me to use our bodies to paint an emotional landscape onstage. I have never been able to explain the alchemy of dance very well—maybe because motion and steps, not the alphabet, are the foundation of the language I speak best. But I could always feel the magic when the dancing and the music emulsified (to use a cooking expression) to create an entirely new artistic and emotional experience, and I loved the process of getting there. In fact, the process was itself the miracle.

Sadly—and, in retrospect, almost comically—during this period when my reputation as a principal dancer and my partnering experiences onstage seemed to be hitting new highs, my partnering adventures offstage were hitting new lows. I remember some dance critic commenting during this period that I performed with "more focus" when I was partnering. I'm not sure that I appreciate or agree with this assessment of my dancing, but the statement certainly applies to my private life. I am one of those people who seems to do much better in a steady relationship with one person. My breakup with Ulrik had been long overdue, but this did not mean that when it finally happened I landed in a happier and more well-adjusted place. On the contrary. The combination of having almost no time for a personal life and very little experience at "playing the field" resulted in a sequence of ill-advised romances that I sometimes refer to as "My Mistakes."

Probably everybody has some passage in their romantic history that makes them cringe to recall. When I look back on this period of my life, my catalog of cringe-worthy mistakes goes something like this: the Screamer, the Architect, the Hollywood Agent, the Wannabe Pop Star, the Famous Painter, the Gossip Columnist, and the Velvet Mogul. Summarizing it so coldly makes it sound like I was doing a brisk business, but most of these encounters were very brief. With the Screamer, for instance, I knew it was a no-go from the moment I had to cover his mouth—which, as I recall, was before we had even begun to undress. The Architect was handsome and older than I, but dating various people at once, which is not my style. The Hollywood Agent and I were never really dating per se, but he was amusing, and he seemed to like to stare at me, which gratified my ego. It seems worth mentioning here that many dancers, even though they are part of a profession that depends on grace and beauty, do not think of themselves as uniquely attractive. This has certainly been true of me—I have always been, and will always be, insecure about my looks. In 1990, *People* magazine included me in its annual roundup of the "50 Most Beautiful People in the World"—but my attitude about this was, What does *People* magazine know? I assumed they had to fill their performing-arts quota for the annual list that year. Over time I have trained myself to look into a mirror without really seeing myself. I look for form and posture in an abstract and artistic evaluation of movement, without seeing my specific body.

The Velvet Mogul was the last—and by far my favorite—in the list of my so-called mistakes, and only a mistake in the sense that I think we both knew before we began that there was no way we would be together forever. We met at a Calvin Klein show and became infatuated with each other, but our ages, backgrounds, and lifestyles were just too disparate for things to work out long term. I had been around plenty of wealthy people during my years at NYCB, but none matched the grand scale on which the Mogul operated. If I was on tour, or if he was out of town, he would sometimes send his plane to fetch me, and he liked to literally shower me with gifts. All of this was really fun, and a little crazy, but what I liked most about the Mogul was that he was always very kind, and he always treated me with the utmost respect. He was a truly good and intelligent person, with a really big and generous heart. We got along.

During the period when I was seeing the Velvet Mogul, I began touring the country during my time off from the company, performing with several of my fellow dancers as part of a special group Heather had organized. Heather had designed excellent programs that the audiences seemed to love, and these tours were generally wild and fun road trips in which we got to travel together, not to mention make some very welcome extra cash. Sometimes the Mogul would send his plane to pick me up from wherever I was dancing on these tours—Lincoln, Nebraska, or Palm Springs, or Miami—and then I would grab Lourdes, Heather, Damian, or whoever was around, and while the rest of the troupe got on a bus to head to the next venue, we would fly out to Beverly Hills or some other place for a few days of fun. It was always amazing to disembark from the plane and find the Mercedes limos waiting for us on the tarmac. People who have that kind of money really do live differently, and it was a kick to go along for the ride for a while—but even as it was happening I knew such a life would not work for me over the long haul. It wasn't long before we broke up, and while we didn't speak for a while afterward, in the long run we have remained cordial. Whenever our paths cross it is always nice to see him. He is a good man, and I wish him well.

The truth of the matter is that although I made what I consider a number of dating mistakes, there was truly no one who would have been an appropriate partner for me at that particular time in my life. What I needed was time alone—something I had never really had since hooking up with Ulrik at age fifteen—and time to figure out where I stood in my dancing career. Some big and daunting changes were looming in the not so distant future—no one talked about it much, but we all knew they were coming. I had reached an age when I couldn't just wing it and bounce through life with the blithe, carefree, *que será, será* reflexes that had served me so well from childhood through my early twenties. I needed to pull back, find myself, think things through, and try to make intelligent plans.

One of the saddest and most difficult experiences during this period of my life, and also a major factor in my general feeling of confusion and doom, came when I learned that my former boyfriend John had been diagnosed with AIDS. AIDS is such a cruel disease, and it had taken so many special

people in our world already. For any gay man there was also
always the constant fear factor—would this awful and unpredictable disease get you, too? By then everyone was well
aware of the AIDS threat, and everyone I knew who was gay
got tested regularly and we were all very careful. But the disease is an insidious and ruthless enemy. I have always been
very lucky, but many others have not been so lucky. It was
heart-wrenching to watch John growing weaker and weaker
over the months, and on the day he finally died I was absolutely flattened with grief. I was scheduled to dance Jerry
Robbins's *The Cage* with Heather that evening, but at 7 p.m.
I was still in my bed, unable to think or move. Our ballet was
the second on the program, and at some point, as time was
running out, Heather called me.

"Honey, you have to get out of bed," Heather said gently.
"Get out of bed and come to the theater." When I got to the
theater, Heather was already in her wig and makeup, waiting
for me in my dressing room. She sat me down and wet my
makeup sponge and began to apply my makeup for me. *The
Cage* is about a Queen (of the insect world) who is teaching
a Novice (Heather) how to seduce her intruders and then kill
them. I was dancing the part of the Second Intruder, whom
the Novice happens to fall in love with, before killing. I remember lying on the floor after the pas de deux with Heather,
staring up into her eyes just before she has to kill me, and
wondering at the strange and sad turns life can take—and
at the powerful imperatives of performance. I was about to
have my neck broken and get stomped to pieces by Heather
in an artistic portrayal of a death onstage at Lincoln Center.
A very dear friend of mine and Heather's had just died, in real

life—and there we were, dancing a fake death. No matter what, the show must always go on.

Life was getting more serious. Everyone was older and everything was changing. Peter Martins and Darci Kistler married in 1991, Heather and Damian were settled into a cozy relationship, and Heather, Damian, and I had become an inseparable trio. I think the three of us were all ready for something new and were craving more stability at the same time, and in 1993 we realized that as a result of our freelance tours around the country we had amassed enough cash collectively to take an extraordinary step that would placate our urges for both novelty and stability. Joining forces with another great friend, Hamilton South, we bought a country house in upstate Connecticut and set about creating the domestic pitter-patter of a "normal" life and home. When Hamilton decided that he wanted a private homestead of his own, Heather and Damian and I bought him out and quickly regrouped as a solid little trio of happy homemakers.

We were the owners of a beautiful home on twenty acres of land, and although our dance schedules did not allow us to spend long stretches there, we did manage to have wonderful times whenever we could get there. Heather and Damian took up gardening with a vengeance, and set about creating a paradise with acres of glorious flowers and bushes and trees. Heather and I launched into a serious cooking phase, and began inviting friends to regular dinner parties at our bucolic retreat. In the winter when it snowed we would sled down the hill all the way to the end of the driveway. In the spring the tulips would arrive in abundance, and in the summer we would sit on the terrace and watch the sunset while our dogs—we had golden retrievers, mine was named Absolut and theirs was named Q—cavorted on the lawn.

As idyllic as our Connecticut homesteading seemed on the surface, over time I think all three of us could feel a spider's web of tensions being spun between us on other levels. It was a complex situation that I'm sure some shrink would have a field day dissecting—a sort of poor man's *Hamlet*. Heather and Peter, my surrogate mother and father, had split and now Heather was with Damian, one of the company's up-and-coming talents. For years Heather and I had been unbelievably close, but every day Heather and Damian were growing closer and closer. They were a heterosexual couple, while I was a single and, at that particular moment, roving gay man. But bigger and more unspoken than any of these conflicts was another huge and frightening change that we all knew was looming: Heather was closing in on forty-one. She had many other interests tugging at her—she had been designing costumes, working incredibly hard with the nonprofit organization God's Love We Deliver, gardening, cooking, and writing. In the fall of 1994, she went to Peter and told him she had decided it was time to retire.

I was horrified at the thought of dancing without Heather, and that last season with her was very emotional and tough. I couldn't believe she was leaving, just like that. It seemed impossible. I had watched dancers retire before, but this was different. Heather was a ballerina whom I'd watched with awe since I first got into the company, marveling at her combinations of edginess and smoothness and the way she manipulated complex movements to create a surreal beauty. Heather was the gifted partner with whom I now danced to create the same kind of surreal beauty in dozens of ballets. She was at the center of my career and my art, and I felt we were at our prime. And now she was going to step down, just turn the faucet off and shut down her magic. I could see that the decision made sense for her, but it terrified me.

The night of Heather's retirement performance, January 15, 1995, was one of the saddest and most emotional nights I ever experienced. We danced Balanchine's *Bugaku* and Peter's *Valse Triste*, and we danced them well—but I was trying so hard not to cry the entire time we were performing. I wanted every moment to last a lifetime. I remember running offstage after our last steps together and bringing armloads of roses back to her and bowing on one knee. We had had fifteen years of dancing together, and of being great friends offstage as well—it was fully half my life at that point. A long, long time. When I looked up I saw tears glistening in Heather's eyes, too, and I saw that she was still in every way and in every moment exactly what Balanchine had once called her: his "wild orchid."

Life takes some very strange turns, and one of the strangest in my case has been that for the past several years, Heather and I, who were once so close, have not spoken much. Over time the two of us have had so many experiences together, and now life has taken us each in our own direction. But one thing we will always have is our memories of our performances together. Those special moments onstage, the great premieres and the opening nights, will never fade. And as long as I live I also will never forget the day of my own retirement, ten years after Heather's, and the look on Heather's face and the tears in her eyes as she threw me flowers from the audience. She threw roses, a big beautiful bouquet of pink and yellow and white roses that she and Damian had grown in the garden of the Connecticut house we once shared.

As I think back to the years when Heather and Damian and I were trying to make a cozy family nest for ourselves in the Connecticut countryside, I am once again haunted by questions about where my real family was nesting during the same years. For the most part, their visits had remained as rare as ever, but at one point during this period their no-madic ramblings brought them east, and they decided to settle in Mashantucket, Connecticut. We were all excited at the prospect of seeing one another more regularly, and they actually did visit me several times at the country house that Heather and Damian and I shared. We spent both the Fourth of July and the following Christmas together there that year, and I remember that for me it was strange—and in many ways stressful—to suddenly have family present at these major holidays. Old tensions that had been dormant for years quickly came to life. One example that stands out oc-curred during their Christmas visit, on Christmas Day. My mother was wearing a pretty, all-white outfit, and just as we were sitting down to Christmas dinner my father turned to her and announced that she looked like a fat marshmallow. I got so angry that I screamed at Pop and insisted he apologize. Mom and I were both always watching our weight, and my strong reaction may have been because, in part, I took the "fat marshmallow" comment personally. But a more impor-tant factor in my anger was the long-standing feelings I had toward my father. Given his performance as a husband, in my opinion my father had no right to criticize my mother, ever, about anything. Whatever my reasons for yelling at my father back then, the memory of that moment breaks my heart now. I saw him so rarely, and for everyone's sake I wish I had controlled my temper.

Shortly after that Christmas visit, my parents hit the road again, heading back to points west and resuming their restless travels, and our experiment with living near one another was officially over. Curious to know where they had come from before that short Connecticut stint, and where they went afterward, I decided to consult my mother's computer files. The answers I found to the blanks in my memory surprised and touched me. Before coming to Connecticut my parents had been working as managers of a mobile home park in Arvada, Colorado, and then as managers of the Gig Harbor RV Resort in the state of Washington. "Joe and Jo are self-starters, dependable, consistent, energetic and resourceful organizers. Both are effective communicators, friendly and recognize priorities and work well together to meet deadlines," my mother wrote in her introduction to their joint résumé. It was after these two stints that Mom and Pop moved to Mashantucket, Connecticut, and when they left Connecticut they went west again, where they lived in Many Farms, Arizona; Gallup, New Mexico; Canutillo, Texas; Pasadena, California; and Santa Fe, New Mexico. And these are only the stops that made it into Mom's résumé.

Reading my mother's résumé filled in more than the geographic blanks in my memory. I learned all sorts of things about what she had been doing while I was dancing my heart out in New York and playacting as landed gentry at my new property in upstate Connecticut. In Mashantucket,

Mom worked with the Mashantucket Pequot Tribal Elders, as an arts-and-crafts and Native regalia researcher and instructor; in Many Farms, Arizona—the same valley where her father had grown his famous tomatoes so many years ago—she submitted a proposal, received approval, raised $285,000 in funding, and founded a nonprofit organization called the Many Farms Senior Wellness Center. In addition to her long list of standard office and secretarial skills, Mom notes her expertise in "native regalia, sewing machines and other sewing methods, bead work, kiln work, paints and other arts and crafts."

Once again I am humbled by the breadth and energy behind my mother's many accomplishments, and reminded of the truth in the opening sentence of the book she never got to write: "One never really gets to know one's parents." As I examine my own life I am beginning to feel that I took everything for granted when I was growing up. I spoiled myself and had the strangest notions of grandeur and poverty. To me, the reservation and the life people led there always seemed poor and sad. Only now am I beginning to realize how rich it actually is—rich with culture, rich with natural beauty, rich with tradition. The house I shared with Heather and Damian in Connecticut may have looked fancy and rich, but did I ever really feel nourished there the way my mother was nourished by her land and her heritage? It is hard to say. I do know I would give anything to sit down and have just one more Christmas dinner with both my white-marshmallow mother and my salsa-singing father (at whom I hope I will never again scream).

Christmas Cheer for Orphans and Strays

FOR DECADES OF my life, the annual run of Balanchine's beloved *Nutcracker* ballet put the kibosh on any out-of-town holiday travel—we dancers got Christmas Day off, period—so every Thanksgiving and Christmas I was inevitably an orphan-guest at the holiday dinners of some kindhearted family in New York. John Gruen and Jane Wilson wrapped me into their family holiday meals on many occasions when I was young, as did Peter and Heather and several other company members who were grown up enough to actually have homes.

These days the NYCB is dark on both Christmas Eve and Christmas Day—such a luxury! But there are still plenty of dancers and colleagues of Luis's from his busy restaurant and sommelier worlds who can't make it home or who have nowhere to go, so every year we put together a dinner for a random assortment of orphans and strays. This is always one of my favorite parties of the year, because we never know who will fill the chairs. What will be on the table is more predictable: a groaning board of standard holiday side dishes and a big old spiral-cut smoked ham. When it comes to gifts they always say it's the thought that counts, so if you are hosting a crowd of unknown size for Christmas, why not think of something easy and give yourself the gift of time?

I always try to keep every other aspect of this meal simple too. For hors d'oeuvres I go to the Chelsea Market and put together a big platter of cheeses, salami, and crudités. For flowers I buy bunches of red roses at the corner deli the night before and keep them in a bucket of warm water—a trick Heather taught me. Just before the guests arrive I cut the stems short (about four inches) and arrange the roses in stemless wineglasses or jelly jars down the center of the table. A couple of big candles and some holly sprigs here and there, some classic holiday music in the background, and a tray of glasses filled with rosé champagne to greet guests as they arrive—with friends like these who needs family?

World's Easiest Christmas Ham

SERVES 10 GENEROUSLY, WITH LEFTOVERS

This really has to be the easiest dish in the world. I like to get a Cook's spiral-sliced hickory-smoked honey ham, but there are many variations of the same. Usually the glaze comes glued to the side of the packaged ham, and instructions (which may vary) are printed on the inside—so remember not to throw the wrapper away too soon.

1 10-pound spiral-sliced hickory-smoked honey ham,
  with glaze packet

Preheat the oven to 275 degrees. Put the ham flat-side down in a large roasting pan, pour the juices from the package the ham came in over the meat, and cover it with aluminum foil. Put the ham in the oven. Let it cook for 2 hours without touching it. At this point, if there is a lot of juice at the bottom of the pan, I pour half of it out, and then baste the ham with the remaining juice. Spread half of the glaze from the glaze packet over the ham, put the aluminum foil back on, and cook for another 50 minutes. Finally, spread the remaining glaze over the ham and cook for another 10 minutes without the aluminum-foil cover. Remove from the oven and let the ham rest, covered with foil, until ready to serve.

This ham makes a perfect entrée for a Christmas crowd, but it's just as good in spring, with some gorgeous asparagus in balsamic vinaigrette. Or serve it for a Sunday brunch with garlic bread, so guests can put their ham between two luscious garlicky crusts and chomp away.

CHAPTER THIRTEEN

Endings Beget Beginnings

Dancing is just discovery, discovery, discovery.
—MARTHA GRAHAM

After that sad January evening in 1995 when I danced my final *Bugaku* and *Valse Triste* with Heather, I was completely lost. It still seemed impossible that she was gone, and I felt totally alone and exposed. Heather and I had been dancing together for so long, and we knew each other so well, both on- and offstage—I wasn't sure there would be much of me left up there onstage without her. I was thirty and I was beginning to feel my years—we boys do all the lifting, and over time our joints pay the price. I had been suffering from more aches and more injuries with each passing year, and in the winter of 1995, as I confronted the prospect of my first season without Heather, I honestly wondered if it might be time for me to retire as well. I thought about this quite seriously, the big question being, of course, what else could I do?

Heather and Damian and I still shared the house in Connecticut, and we would hole up there together whenever we could, doing our best to maintain the work-hard, play-hard lifestyle we had led before. Heather and I launched a new partnership when we began to work together on a cookbook that would present some of our favorite meals. This gave us a comforting transitional partnering mode, but in truth the basic frame beneath our rolling adventure had changed—two of us were still performing in Lincoln Center every night, while one of us was moving on to explore new territory. The cadence of our days, the rhythm of our professional responsibilities, had been altered—and as time passed everything else began to change, too.

One inevitable change resulting from Heather's retirement was that I began to partner other ballerinas more frequently, and as a result, my stage rapport with various company members began to open up and expand. Of course everyone in the company dances with one another in all kinds of combinations, and over the years I had had the privilege of partnering many astoundingly talented ballerinas. But my partnership with Heather, in the final years before she retired, had become such an intense and defining aspect of my professional life that it had overshadowed most other experiences. In some situations my closeness to Heather even complicated matters. Relations between Heather and Darci, for instance, had always been a little distant—not just because Peter had been involved with each of them, but also because of fundamental differences in their personalities and styles. After Heather's retirement, Peter began casting me with Darci more often, and I was pleased when a deeper friendship began to develop between us.

Another ballerina I began to dance with more and more by this time was the supremely talented and intensely dedicated

Wendy Whelan. Wendy had joined the company in 1986 and had been promoted to principal in 1991. In February, the month after Heather retired, Wendy and I danced the premiere of Dick Tanner's *Operetta Affezionata*, and we were extremely comfortable together onstage. Over time Wendy began to take over some of the roles Heather had always danced with me, and slowly I could feel a special rapport, almost like a new language, beginning to develop between us as we performed. By the end of that year—a year that had started with me seriously considering retirement—I looked back and realized that I had premiered four new ballets: Tanner's *Operetta Affezionta*, Kevin O'Day's *Huoah*, Jerry Robbins's revival of *West Side Story Suite*, and Peter Martins's *Adams Violin Concerto*. In the fall I traveled with the company to Paris to dance for two weeks at the International Festival de Danse de Paris. Maybe I wasn't completely washed up after all—in fact, I realized, I felt invigorated and very enthusiastic about the future.

One of the reasons for my enthusiasm and optimism may have been a new relationship—one that would affect both my personal and professional lives—that was just beginning at about this time. To trace this relationship back to its roots, I have to go back to an evening in 1993 when I was dancing Robbins's *Afternoon of a Faun*. A couple of times while I was performing this ballet I had the strange feeling of being watched intensely by someone in the wings—anyone who has been onstage knows this feeling. When I looked over I saw a young dancer named Christopher Wheeldon, a former member of the Royal Ballet in London who had recently joined the NYCB, staring intently at me. For my role in *Faun* I wore tights and no shirt, and I remember wondering briefly if it was possible that this boy had a crush on me. No, I decided.

My next encounter with Chris came quite a while later when the company was in residence in Saratoga. I was in transit between rehearsals for my own ballets, passing through the main rehearsal hall, where ballet master Victor Castelli was rehearsing *Dances at a Gathering*. Chris was dancing the Giggle Boy part of *Dances*, a passage where he had to lift Wendy Whelan. He was having some trouble lifting Wendy all the way, and as I passed, Victor stopped the rehearsal and called out to me.

"Jock!" he said. "Can you help Chris with this lift? He's having trouble. What should he do?"

It was a hideously hot and humid day, and I was sweating like a pig and already late for my next rehearsal. I looked at them, and the first words to fall out of my mouth were "Well, he should do some push-ups." Then I walked out of the rehearsal studio without another word. That was our first exchange—what a bitch I was.

My next significant encounter with Chris was not until 1995, in New York, when Lourdes Lopez and I were warming up for a ballet—I think it was *Midsummer Night's Dream*—that Chris was dancing in too. Between our passages onstage Lourdes and I wound up talking about Chris, and I admitted that I thought he was very talented and "kind of cute." The truth is, by this time I knew a little more about Chris, and I was intrigued. I was attracted to his boyishness, of course, but I could also feel how eager and driven he was. He was a beautiful dancer, with beautiful legs and feet, but he also had great ambition and potential as a choreographer. I had seen some of the work he had choreographed for the SAB, and it was very, very good. In many ways he reminded me of Damian, who had already choreographed some pieces for both the school and the company; they were both go-getters with big talents and big visions. They both had that special aura that radiates from people who you know are going to become exactly what they want to become.

I was attracted to all of these qualities in Chris, but given my recent history of bad romantic choices, I was not really in the market for a boyfriend. In fact, I was somewhat aghast that night when Lourdes called Chris over and asked him what he was doing after the performance. I just stared at her—what was she doing? Chris said he had no plans, and when Lourdes pressed him to join the two of us for dinner, he agreed. It was, essentially, my first date with Chris—engineered not by either Chris or me, but by the dynamic Lourdes Lopez.

Sometimes it shocks me to think about what a kid Chris was when we got together. He was twenty-two and I was thirty. I had always been the one who dated older men, but in this case I guess the passage of time kind of turned the tables on me. Not long after we got together Chris moved into my apartment, and we ended up living together for the next six years. Those years proved to be a hugely important period of my life—perhaps most significantly in terms of the professional collaboration that evolved between the two of us. I knew that Chris had been brought up in the Royal Ballet and was a true classicist—he was a Kenneth MacMillan fan. But I also knew he believed Balanchine was a genius, and that he harbored a hunger for Balanchine's invention and freshness. I was attracted to Chris's obvious talent and understood his desire to create ballets that combined a feeling of innovation and classicism. It seems quite likely that Chris's attraction to me was also at least in part professionally motivated—I was an experienced and established dancer who by then had been choreographed on many times by many artists. We sensed that we could help each other learn and grow, and while I take no credit for Chris's choreography, I do feel that we were both right. We did work well together. In the ballets for which Wendy Whelan joined Chris and me as a third partner in this collaborative process, the experience expanded into something truly sublime.

Although Chris and I may have sensed the potential in our professional collaboration from the beginning, this was not something we were able to explore immediately. For one thing, in November 1995, shortly after Chris and I got together, I suffered one of the worst injuries of my career. I was dancing Balanchine's *Allegro Brillante*, a very intense and fiendishly fast ballet, and during my final leap in the second entrance with Wendy I felt a stab of pain and heard a sickening pop—I had torn a calf muscle. As I exited to the wings, limping, I knew there was no way I could dance the next entry. I screamed to Damian, who was warming up for his own ballet later that evening, and explained the situation, and then limped back onstage for an ensemble passage that I knew I could fake my way through. When Wendy began the solo that leads into the next pas de deux, I exited with the rest of the corps. Damian, wearing his warm-up tights under a tunic he had grabbed from somewhere backstage, heroically leaped in and took over my part. His rescue was so smooth and seamless.

That torn calf muscle was my first really serious injury—dancing is a very risky business, and I was comparatively lucky not to have had a major injury earlier—and it gave me a foretaste of the frustrations to come. My roles were severely curtailed for the next year as I worked on getting my calf back to strength, and it was not until 1997 that I had fully recovered. But there were some upsides from that year of reduced dancing, one of which was that because I had more time on my hands, at Peter's suggestion, in 1996 I began teaching some classes at SAB for the first time. It is strange to think back and remember how nervous and uncomfortable I was with these duties in the beginning—no doubt because I was insecure and unsure of my abilities as a teacher. Now I love teaching, so much that I cannot imagine not having it as part of my life. Another upside of dancing less was that I could devote more time to the new project Heather and I were working on together. After toying with the idea for some time, we were working seriously on a cookbook based on the informal dinners and gatherings we cohosted for friends. In 1997 we managed to complete our book, and published it with Riverhead Press under the title *Our Meals*.

It was not until I fully recovered from my injury, in the spring of 1997, that Chris and I began our collaboration in earnest, when Peter asked him to choreograph his first ballet for the company on me and Monique Meunier. It was called *Slavonic Dances*, and in addition to Monique and me, it featured a big corps. I was impressed by how crafty and inventive Chris was about using a big corps, and I think he was grateful for the ways I was able to help him with some of the partnering passages. *Slavonic Dances* was one of six new ballets created for the annual Diamond Project that spring, and it would be one of three ballets chosen to premiere that summer at Saratoga. I remember Chris and I were both insanely busy at that time—he was dancing as a soloist with the company and also choreographing, and I was dancing four premieres in the month of June alone: Chris's *Slavonic Dances*, Peter Martins's *Them Twos*, Miriam Mahdaviani's *Urban Dances*, and Robert La Fosse's *Concerto in Five Movements*. In fact, it was probably a good thing Chris and I enjoyed our professional collaboration so much, because we had very little time to explore much of anything else. We did go to South America together that fall when one group of company dancers went on tour in the Pacific Rim while a second group—including Chris and me—toured Brazil. My main memory of that trip is that everyone in our group ate a little too much Brazilian food and drank a few too many caipirinhas, and as a result we all waddled home a little fatter than when we had left.

The following January marked the beginning of the company's fiftieth anniversary, and the launch of a series of special celebrations and performances at home and around the country. As always, Peter Martins was brainstorming a number of new ballets that year, with a wide range of feeling to them, and I was lucky enough to work with him on two pieces—*River of Light* and *Stabat Mater*—that were wildly different. The former was a stark and futuristic ballet set to a Charles Wuorinen score, and showcased the special talent Peter has for finding and expressing incredible beauty and grace embedded in a passage of music that can be difficult to count and even unappealing to the ear initially. Three couples danced in virtual rivers of light created by lighting designer Mark Stanley, and when Darci and I performed our final pas de deux we danced inside a ring of light that seemed to be floating in the water. *Stabat Mater*, by contrast, had a feeling of great antiquity and classicism, and featured three couples who come to life amid what appear to be Greek ruins. Peter created *Stabat* as a somber and moving tribute to the amazing ballet teacher Stanley Williams, who after thirty-seven years with the SAB, had died the previous fall. Stanley was renowned worldwide, and he taught so many of us so brilliantly. I remember I was driving uptown to take Stanley's class when my cell phone rang. It was Heather. She said, "Jock, are you going to class?" I said, "Yes, I'm going to class." Then she said, "Well, prepare yourself. Stanley died this morning." I was stunned, but I just kept going. I drove to the school, I parked, I walked upstairs, I changed, and I headed into the studio. Everyone else in the class had done the same thing—we were all so upset, but we didn't know what else to do. Somebody said, "Peter's going to teach." Then Peter Martins walked in and said, "Stanley would have wanted this." Then Peter started teaching.

Stanley's death was a blow to the school and to the company, and to the dance world at large. It was followed by another sad milestone in July 1998 when Jerome Robbins died. He was seventy-nine and had been very ill, and it had almost felt as if he might have been waiting to see NYCB reach its fifty-year birthday before letting go. Jerry had been such a force in my career and in the company overall—a genius as a choreographer and always so intense during rehearsals. I will always especially remember our rehearsals in 1995 for his groundbreaking *West Side Story Suite*, in which I danced the part of Bernardo, leader of the Sharks, and Nikolaj Hübbe danced Riff, leader of the Jets. Jerry had choreographed this work for Broadway, but it had never been performed by a ballet company before, which made the project both exciting and ambitious. And demanding. I remember Jerry screaming at all of us, insisting that we had to confront one another with more passion, and begin to show a real hatred for one another, as rival gang members would. We were nervous and insecure and jittery under his eye, and his tactics could be so brutal. One day, when Lourdes Lopez and I were rehearsing the gym scene together, Jerry arrived, leading a Broadway star by the hand, and he came toward me and then just slipped her hand into mine. Out of the corner of my eye I saw Lourdes pick up her bag and leave the room. I wanted to cry, I felt so bad for her. But she wasn't the first dancer he had done that to—Jerry was Jerry.

A few weeks later, Nik and I came in for rehearsal and in the dressing room we decided we had really had it with the way Jerry was treating us and the whole cast. We decided that if he screamed at either one of us that day, or at anyone, we would walk out of the room and never return. He had pushed our last button. We walked into the rehearsal room together and stood in the back. When everyone else had finally arrived, Jerry told us all to sit down. Nik and I remained in the back, leaning against the barre.

Jerry started to talk about the importance of our roles, how we had to become the characters we were portraying. Then he looked up and pointed to Nik and me and said,

"Everyone in this room has to come up to Jock's and Nikolaj's level. Everyone has to become a true Shark or Jet." Nik and I felt our anger deflate; all of our resentment just disappeared. All of those rehearsals when Jerry had been so frightening and so mean faded away. It was almost as if the savvy old beast knew he had pushed us as far as he could, as if he knew we were about to walk out. In the end, I have to say, dancing *West Side Story Suite* was truly one of the best experiences I ever had. Jerry was a true genius, and I am so grateful I got to work with him.

We all mourned the passing of these two amazing men, whose talents had been so essential to the spirit and execution of Balanchine's vision. At the same time, I felt that I had a front-row seat at the birth of another impressive choreographic talent that had the potential to carry the vision forward—my boyfriend, Chris. In 1999, Chris choreographed *Scènes de Ballet* for the company, which featured more than sixty students from the SAB, and then in 2000 he choreographed another ballet, *Mercurial Manoeuvres*, on Miranda Weese and me. Miranda was a creature of great gifts, strikingly beautiful with long black hair and an intense presence. She had studied Heather's footwork very carefully over the years, training a close eye on every move, and her homework had paid off. She had very precise, intelligent, quiet feet that could not take a bad step. At first when we were dancing together Miranda was trying to do everything, leaping and jumping and trying to muscle her way through the steps. I had to say, "Stop working so hard. You'll hurt me. Let me do the work." Once she understood what I meant, and realized that I could in fact put her wherever she needed to be, we danced beautifully together. There was a quietness—almost a quality of stealth—and a musicality about Miranda's dancing that met and enhanced the same qualities in my own.

Mercurial Manoeuvres was more complex and intriguing than Chris's previous works, and the intricate counts and interweaving of modern and classic steps definitely foreshadowed things to come. There was a moment in the middle of our pas de deux when Miranda and I just looked into each other's eyes for about eight slow counts. Damian later told me he thought it was one of the most beautiful moments in ballet history. No movement, just music playing and bodies breathing, souls staring into each other. A moment in time. I found it thrilling to be participating in the creation of something that felt like the beginning of a new and fresh form of expression in ballet.

Later that year, Chris retired as a dancer to concentrate more exclusively on choreography, and he accepted a position that Peter offered him—the first of its kind at the NYCB—as artist in residence. In August he and I took one of our rare vacations together—and one that I feel marked a turning point in our relationship as collaborators—when we went to visit his family in England. At the time I was trying to encourage Chris to move away from the pure classical idiom, to find the courage to step forward and explore his yearning for something newer and fresher. I wanted him to attempt sleeker creations, to strip away costumes and sets and evoke emotions through the manipulation of movement and physical steps as Balanchine had in breathtaking ballets like *Episodes* and *The Four Temperaments* and the wonderful *Agon*. While we were staying in London we went to the Royal Academy of Arts to see a traveling exhibit of sensationalist art called Apocalypse, and the two of us ended up getting separated and wandered through on our own, each of us fascinated by different aspects of the exhibitions. (I remember one was a strange representation of the pope pinned to the ground by a meteorite.) When we got back to our hotel room we were both excited by what we had seen, and we decided to listen to a CD we had picked up at Tower Records on the way home. It was piano music by a composer Chris had recently fallen in love with— György Ligeti—and we laughed when we realized that one of the pieces on the CD had been used over and over in a really annoying way in the sound track of the recently released film *Eyes Wide Shut*. I didn't especially care for Ligeti's music at first, but the more I listened, the more I liked it. Finally I turned to Chris and said, "All you have to do is, when we get back to New York take me and Wendy Whelan into a room with this music and see what happens. Who could be more pliable and creative than Wendy?" When we got back to New York this was precisely what we did—and that was the beginning of Chris's brilliant ballet *Polyphonia*. It was also the beginning of a new and exciting collaboration: Wheeldon, Whelan, and me.

WHEN CHRIS FIRST started making *Polyphonia* for Wendy and me and three other couples, I didn't realize how far Chris, Wendy, and I could go as a team, how far we could take ourselves in new directions. I had done a lot of difficult ballets that required stamina, but this one took things to a new level. I was excited by the maturity and complexity of the choreography. As I mentioned, I had felt for some time that Chris needed to get away from frilly ballets and to try new things—and this was definitely new. Working in the studio for hours, he and Wendy and I collaborated on the various pas de deux. Wendy and I had been performing with each other for some time, but these collaborations with Chris gave us a new relationship, a new focus, and a new level of profundity in our partnering. We began to develop a deeper trust in each other, and a deeper understanding of our individual strengths and beliefs, which in turn allowed us to let go of our individual selves and become more like two people in one body. I found it so exciting the way we three could go into a room and create something that really meant something to us, and then bring it to the stage and share it with an audience. The experience gave me a fresh take on what could be done both physically and artistically—it really felt as if we were stepping through a door into whole new territories of dance and choreography—and it also gave me the inspiration and courage to carry on. When you're a male dancer and past the age of thirty you can begin to feel kind of lost. You start asking yourself, What do I do now? Do I continue this or do I quit and do something else? Most dancers quit around forty, or earlier if their bodies can't take it anymore. But as Wendy, Chris, and I began to move forward in new and innovative ways, I felt a rush of energy and passion for my art surging through me, a kind of second wind—which was really pretty remarkable, considering that five years earlier I had been seriously contemplating retirement. I think our collaboration also gave Wendy and Chris the courage and creativity to explore and shape new and exciting identities. Timing is everything in dance, and the three of us had come together at exactly the right time.

When *Polyphonia* premiered, in January 2001, it was very well received, and critics especially praised its "interweaving of ballet and modern dance." Chris really seemed to be hitting his stride when, that May, he was named NYCB's first resident choreographer. That same month Darci and I danced the premiere of *Morgen*—a very beautiful, mature, and emotional ballet made by Peter as a kind of love letter to Darci—and I remember that throughout the choreography sessions and rehearsals for *Morgen* I was excited to sense that Peter and Darci and I were also connecting in new and deeper ways as collaborators. I could never have predicted that all these new and exciting frontiers were coming my way as a dancer, and I felt that I had learned an important lesson, not just about dancing but about life: stay curious and open, and always explore opportunities when they present themselves; you never know what you will discover or where inspiration will come from and how it will shape your life. Sometimes a series of small steps will bring you to the biggest leaps.

I sometimes think of that trip to London and the afternoon that Chris and I spent at the Royal Academy of Arts— wandering about separately and then coming back together to discuss our enthusiasms—as a kind of marker, a moment when the seeds were sewn for a whole new flowering in the collaboration between Chris and me as choreographer and dancer working together. Remembering that trip now also brings back memories of another trip Chris and I took, the summer before our London visit, when we traveled together to visit my family on the reservation in Arizona. The Arizona trip was a very different kind of adventure from our London sojourn but, in retrospect, enlightening in its own way.

To spare Chris the experience of bunking with my parents in their motor home on this trip, I booked the two of us a room in the Thunderbird Lodge—a motel on the reservation, right at the edge of the beautiful Canyon de Chelly. We decided to drive around and explore the area—something that had never occurred to me to do before. Every time we were about to head off on one of our adventures, Mom would approach us and insist that we be back before sundown. Otherwise, she assured us, something bad was going to happen. As the week rolled toward Friday, Mom became more and more adamant about this, and when Friday came she finally explained her concerns to Chris. Every Friday, when they get paid, the Indians drive to Gallup to buy liquor—there is no liquor for sale on the reservation. Then they get drunk and drive home. Because there is only one road to and from the reservation, a lot of people wind up getting killed in alcohol-induced car crashes if they are driving, or by being run over by drunk drivers if they are pedestrians. (This can happen any day of the week, but especially on Fridays.) This is extremely common, Mom explained—in fact, two of Mom's sisters' husbands had been driving together and had been killed in exactly this way, in an alcohol-related car accident on the way back to the reservation. Chris listened to Mom, his eyes getting wider and wider—he was very patient and polite. But the whole situation was a little surreal. I had brought this erudite white English boy to the reservation, where everyone was staring at him.

Sometime much later Chris confessed that his visit to the

reservation had been "both fascinating and terrifying, almost like being on another planet." The landscape must have looked lunar to this boy who had grown up in the rolling countryside of Somerset, England, and even I feel a subtle attitude of guardedness and mistrust directed at me as an "outsider" whenever I am visiting the reservation. The extreme differences between Chris's and my backgrounds strike me as almost comical now. And yet, in the realm of choreography and dance at least, the two of us seemed to make an excellent team.

Seasoning the Guest List for a Spicy Evening

WHEN HEATHER AND I were first dancing together she was the more seasoned dancer—but I was the more experienced cook. Over time we learned from each other and soon enough we had a well-balanced partnership both on the stage and in the kitchen. Our dancing was always all about passion and precision, but for the most part our cooking was a much more slapdash affair—a way to unwind and connect with friends in a casual setting.

Over the years I have learned that a successful dinner party is as much about the personalities one mixes as it is about the edible ingredients one combines. An example that comes to mind is a not so long ago night when my dear friend Johnny Reinhold—the famous jeweler whom I first met during my Andy Warhol days—was coming for dinner. I decided to invite several of the ballet boys to the dinner. I thought this would make Johnny happy. (It did.) I also invited a mystery guest—of course the boys were very curious about whom this might be, but I refused to say.

Luis and I were in the kitchen getting the dinner ready— skirt steak over arugula; rosemary-and-garlic potatoes; tomato, red onion, and blue cheese salad; and apple-cheddar crumble—when suddenly the living room fell silent. I walked out to see that Debbie Harry had arrived. The boys were flabbergasted.

It was great to see Debbie and Johnny again, and to share our memories of life when Andy was alive. After dinner, as a spontaneous finale, all the ballet boys decided to take off their shirts. Everyone went away happy—well fed and well entertained. What more can a host hope for?

Grilled Skirt Steak with Arugula

SERVES 6

THE MARINADE:

½ cup olive oil

¼ cup red wine vinegar

5 cloves garlic, finely
  chopped

2 tablespoons chopped
  fresh rosemary

2 tablespoons chopped
  fresh thyme

1 teaspoon salt

½ teaspoon pepper

THE SKIRT STEAK
WITH ARUGULA:

3 pounds skirt steak

A couple bushels
  (metaphorically)
  arugula, washed and
  dried

Olive oil

Red wine vinegar

Salt and pepper

For the marinade, mix the olive oil, red wine vinegar, garlic, rosemary, thyme, salt, and pepper in a small bowl. Pour the mixture over the steak in a large bowl. Cover and let marinate for 1 to 2 hours, or overnight in the refrigerator. (If you refrigerate the meat, bring it to room temperature before cooking.)

Get your large skillet or grill very hot and sear the steak for about 3 minutes per side. Remove from the heat and let it sit while you prepare your arugula by tossing it with olive oil, red wine vinegar, and salt and pepper to taste. It's really not difficult, just keep tasting and adjusting as you go. Slice your steak into strips, cutting diagonally across the grain, and arrange the strips on a nice plate or platter. I like to place the arugula on top of the steak, right down the center.

NOTE: This recipe is incredibly easy, and you can adjust the seasoning as you like. I have played around with adding Sazón (which you can buy in the international-food section of your market), soy sauce, jalapeños, cumin, Worcestershire sauce, mustard, and other surprise ingredients. I also have been known to wrap the steak and arugula in a tortilla for a quick, delicious snack.

CHAPTER FOURTEEN

To Everything Turn, Turn, Turn

What the caterpillar calls the end of the world,
the master calls a butterfly.
—RICHARD BACH

In August and September 2001 the whole NYCB company set off on a tour through Europe, where we were scheduled to dance first at the Edinburgh Festival in Scotland, then in Athens, and finally in Italy for the Parma Verdi Festival. This marked our first visit to Edinburgh, and we were all very excited to be in the land of fine ales—the moment we got there we hit the pubs. The audiences seemed equally excited to have the NYCB in their city. In Athens we danced for a crowd of five thousand in the ancient amphitheater the Herodeion, with the Acropolis beautifully lit, high on a hill behind us. I had danced "Rubies" at the Acropolis with Heather years earlier, on a private tour, and as I got ready to partner Darci this time—Balanchine's last ballerina—in the second movement of *Symphony in C*, the layers of history and symbolism seemed almost surreal.

But for all the excitement and glamour of our earlier stops, it was our last stop, in Parma, that was by far the most memorable. It was there, while in the middle of an orchestra rehearsal of Peter's *Barber Violin Concerto* with Darci, that I glanced offstage and noticed a few dancers crying. As soon as Darci and I finished the pas de deux, we exited the stage and went over to see what had happened. Monique Meunier told me, "They've attacked the Twin Towers in New York." "They?" I thought. "Who are 'they'?" When the rehearsal was over I remember almost running to the hotel, and as I left the theater I saw news crews already gathering at the stage door. We were the New York City Ballet—the namesake company of a great city that had been attacked by "them." But who were they?

What a tumultuous and emotional time that was for all of us who were so far from home and our loved ones. All of the dancers who had families were sent home first, and the company manager arranged for those of us who stayed in Italy to travel from one town to the next until our flights could be arranged. When I finally returned to New York, ten days after the towers went down, Heather, Chris, and Damian all picked me up at the airport. As we drove back over the Triboro Bridge I could see a cloud of smoke still rising from ground zero. It was chilling. We drove in silence to our apartment, and when I stepped out of the car onto the sidewalk the stench of torn metal and burning rubber crowded up against me. It was such a distinctive smell, clear and vibrant in an odd way, and I couldn't help thinking of all of the dead souls that must be floating overhead, circling the skies above the city, looking for their families and for answers as to why this happened.

I slept badly that night, listening to the warplanes flying their grim patrols. Was this going to be our way of life from now on? Would we ever catch the terrorists who had killed our innocent men and women? Would we ever regain our confidence as New Yorkers, or were we doomed to carry a permanent burden of vulnerability forward into our future?

The feeling of confusion and vulnerability that enveloped New York City during that fall of 2001 was echoed by an ominous and brooding quality in my personal life. Everything seemed to be shifting for Chris and for me, and it was not clear exactly where we would each land. Chris was getting a lot of work outside the ballet world—he had done some work in the film industry, and he had just landed his first Broadway show, *Sweet Smell of Success*, starring John Lithgow, which was in Chicago for its pre-Broadway run. This was a big deal, and he was away a lot. Because of this, and because our professional responsibilities had the two of us moving in different directions, we were seeing even less of each other than usual. Despite this, we had decided to move into a fancy new apartment in a brand-new building at Twenty-fourth Street and Seventh Avenue. When the Christmas season rolled around, I was sitting alone in our new New York apartment and Chris was out in Chicago. Our intermittent telephone conversations were often both tense and brief.

Sometime before New Year's, in one of these telephone conversations, Chris said he had something he wanted to discuss with me, but he wanted to do it in person. My antennae went up immediately. This sounded like classic prelude-to-a-breakup to me—but no one had ever broken up with me before, so I was like, *what*?! I couldn't believe it. I asked him outright, on the spot. I said, "What are you doing? Are you breaking up with me? Over the phone?" He said, "No, no, no, let's discuss this when I get home in a couple of days." So I hung up and went out to dinner with our mutual friend the dancer Jason Fowler, and tried to push the matter out of my mind.

When I got home a few hours later I had a message on my answering machine from a woman who was one of Chris's best friends: "Oh my God, I am so sorry that you guys have broken up. If you need to talk please call me." I was shocked, angry, hurt—but most of all humiliated. This was embarrassing—after all, I was an established principal dancer! And I had just been dumped—via voice mail, by my boyfriend's friend, no less. I was stunned. I erased the awful message and called Chris immediately and read him the riot act. He was horrified, too. Basically his best friend had broken up with me for him, by accident. It was a bumbling mistake. But there it was. And since I have been the author of some pretty poorly executed good-byes in my day, it seemed only fair to describe a time when the tables were turned on me.

In retrospect, I can see that during much of the six years that Chris and I were together I was confused, and often felt as if our connection was more of a professional collaboration than a real relationship. It was hard to figure out exactly what we were to each other, and by the time we split up I think I was more humiliated by the way it had happened than I was heartbroken. I think Chris was also confused about our relationship, and unsure of how to proceed. He had met a lot of people in New York over the years, and he was very talented and driven. He probably began to realize that it's a great, big world and that he didn't have to be locked down with his first serious boyfriend. He explained to me later that he just didn't know how to break up with me, and I can certainly understand this—I had felt the same way at times with Ulrik.

Looking back on that uncomfortable period of my life, I have to admit that I didn't handle my first experience as a dumpee with much grace. I was pretty bitchy to Chris for a while—more out of wounded pride than anything else. When he called me and said, "Look, we really have to talk about this," I said, "There's nothing to talk about." And I hung up. In another phone conversation I announced, like the good angry, scorned Navajo brave that I was, "I curse your next relationship!" He said, "You can't do that." And I said, "Oh yes, I can"—and hung up.

While the end of our romance may not have been heartbreaking for either Chris or me in the long run, it certainly was awkward on several fronts in the short term. For one thing we had just moved into this big, expensive apartment; Chris had bought the apartment with the money from all of the ballets and shows that he was doing, but I owned almost everything in the apartment. Then there was the awkward fact that Chris was starting a new ballet with Wendy and me the following week, and so we knew we would be spending a lot of time in the studio together. The ballet was *Morphoses*, a very clever work that Chris choreographed on me, Wendy, Damian, and Alexandra Ansanelli. It was just the four of us in a studio with Chris for a month and a half before the premiere in June 2002, all of which was very uncomfortable for me at first. But I respected Chris's choreography enormously, and I believe he respected my gifts as a dancer and collaborator—as I've said, it can be hard, but you have to leave your problems outside the studio. Thank God, Chris and I were always able to stay professional when it came to our art.

As it turned out, Chris and I ended up working together on four ballets after the breakup: *Morphoses*, *Liturgy*, *Shambards*, and *After the Rain*. They were all beautiful ballets; in fact, they encompass some of our most interesting work. *Liturgy*, another pas de deux for Wendy and me, was set to a spectacularly beautiful piece of music by Arvo Pärt; the partnering was complex and the music difficult to count, but the result was amazing—sort of like dancing in space. I truly believe we were moving the art of partnering forward, exploring an entirely new realm of expression and connection through movement and music. One of my most unearthly memories is of performing *Liturgy* with Wendy in Moscow, on the severely raked stage of the Bolshoi theater. The audience loved the ballet, and when I exited the theater and looked up at the Kremlin I was overwhelmed by the sheer scale of their city.

After *Liturgy*, Chris made *Shambards*, a beautiful ballet with Miranda Weese and me, set to a score commissioned from composer James MacMillan; and then, finally, the very beautiful *After the Rain*. This was the last ballet Chris choreographed on Wendy and me, and it premiered in January 2005, just six months before I retired. I remember being in the rehearsal studio one day when we were first working on *After the Rain*, which was again set to music by Arvo Pärt, and when the choreography seemed to keep coming out just like that of *Liturgy*, Chris got very frustrated. He called an end to our rehearsal and we all left. The next day we came in and he said, "Wendy, take your hair down and take your pointe shoes off." She was a little nervous, and she said, "I've never done that before. Can I wear my ballet slippers?" Chris said yes, okay. I had done modern ballet before, so I suggested, "I can take my shoes off." I didn't know where Chris was going, but this turned out to be the beginning of a very new and inventive pas de deux—one of the most difficult and most beautiful pas de deux I ever danced. The ballet opens with three couples in unitards, dancing against a beautiful backdrop with everything looking well lit and sleek, but with the ominous feeling of an approaching storm. When Wendy and I go offstage, the music begins to get wilder and wilder as the storm hits, and by the time we run back on, the storm has passed and everything has changed. Wendy has let her hair down and she is in a pink leotard. I have taken my shoes off and am wearing only slacks. All of a sudden an amazing early-morning light suffuses everything, and we are dancing in a new way in a new world—after the rain. It was unexpected and fresh and stunning.

Chris is a very gifted choreographer, but perhaps the greatest gift I received from working with him was the friendship and partnership that I found with Wendy. I have mentioned that I always tell my students at the school that as a dancer you must believe in every step and every gesture that you make, or you will never reach the audience. Wendy is the epitome of this—she believes in every nanosecond of every step and gesture. She is one of the hardest working ballerinas of all time, and certainly one of America's finest ever. What was especially exciting and profound about dancing with Wendy was that we could always stretch each other's range, meeting each other anywhere we went. The ideas, the movement, the shapes she could make were amazing. I could manipulate her body with infinitely different subtleties of movement, and she would sculpt her body in response, bringing beauty and magic to every moment of our partnership, beat by beat. We always danced for and with each other, and in the process it was as if we merged and became one soul. Our steps were an extension of the love we felt for each other, for our art, for what we believed in. I truly believe our partnership was a gift to each of us, and that we helped bring the pas de deux into this century. I wish that life worked in a way that would allow the two of us to keep dancing with each other for centuries to come. Even now whenever I speak to her I tell her, "You know I loves ya." Wendy Whelan—the Hardest Working American Ballerina. This should be shouted from the rooftops, and she deserves to be carried down Broadway every day on a float to the theater. I still miss those moments with her, but I will never forget them.

My professional life continued to thrive in the aftermath of my breakup with Chris, but I personally had been badly shaken by what happened between Chris and me, and I wasn't that interested in another serious long-term affair. To be honest, I wasn't even that interested in dating at all. I was working so hard as a dancer—and the process takes a lot more out of you as you get older. Often I would go to the house in Connecticut on the weekends just to collapse and recoup. That spring, when I had some time off, my friend Jason and I thought we really should try to have some fun, so we decided to go on a Gay Holiday. We just drove through Texas, stopping at all the gay bars in Houston and Austin. Next we drove to Dallas to visit Jason's parents, and then we flew back to New York. The whole thing was kind of scary—scary, and exhausting.

During this post-Chris period I had a string of halfhearted dating blunders, similar to the list of mistakes I had dated during my first "love sabbatical"—this time it was the Bartender, the Architect, the Doctor, the Agent, the Narcoleptic (was I really *that* boring?), and the Catholic. The Catholic was the last of these ill-suited suitors, as well as the last straw for me. He was a big, handsome guy who would come watch me dance and then take me out to dinner—over and over. Like an idiot I stuck around, until the night he took me to Peter Luger's in Brooklyn for my birthday. We're sitting there, having dinner; they bring me my cake; everybody sings; and as he tucks into his cake, the Catholic tells me he is having a tough time because he is torn between me and a flight attendant—oh, and a guy he's been breaking up with for six months.

I just stared at him. "You don't get to have *three* people," I said quietly. "You get to have *one*."

He sighed and said, "God will help me through this."

"No. God is *not* going to help you through this," I said. "I am." And that was the end of the Catholic—and of my dating career, as it happens. I just gave up. It was too depressing, too tawdry, and I had other, more pressing things to worry about. My body, for instance. I was getting injured more and more frequently, and I had so many aches and pains from years and years of dancing and lifting ballerinas and generally pushing myself physically. I was spending a lot of time with physical therapists Marika Molnar and Michelle Rodriguez, and with my body trainers Declan Condron and Michelle Khai, and with the miracle-worker chiropractor Larry DeMann Jr., who took care of many of us at the NYCB. But it was tough.

I had another disturbing problem that I didn't like to talk

about much back then, or even now. For a long time the pesky ghost who had stalked me during my childhood years had remained mercifully absent, but somewhere in my midthirties she returned. At first I tried to ignore her. I told myself that the whole notion of being haunted by a ghost was a silly hallucination left over from my childhood. But this particular ghost was determined and persistent. I could sense her near me more and more at different times during the night and day—slipping into rooms right behind me, tailing me on my subway commute in the morning, sliding into mirrors just after I had turned away, and staring fiercely at my departing back. I tried to tell myself that even if she was there, she was harmless—but the situation made me increasingly anxious. My mother sent me some of the special sacred cornmeal, and I dutifully sprinkled it around the doors and windows to protect myself. I remember there was one night, when Chris and I were still together, when I was too petrified by the approaching ghost to even move, and poor Chris had to call my mother and get directions on how to distribute the cornmeal.

I sprinkled cornmeal and tried to ignore my strange shadow, but over time she seemed to be getting more and more aggressive. In the spring of 2003 my ghost—or the witch, as she seemed to me to have become by this time— followed me all the way to Binghamton, New York, when I had a dancing engagement there. After the performance that night she crawled into my hotel bed and curled up against me. She had become more than annoying. She was ruining my sleep, wearing me out, and throwing me off-balance. When I told my mother about the situation she insisted that it was time for me to make a trip to the reservation to see our medicine man, a relative whom we always called Uncle Joe. Reluctantly, I agreed.

I always feel caught in the middle when it comes to Navajo traditions and spiritual practices—I feel I can neither dismiss them nor surrender entirely to them. All Navajo ceremonies tend to be long and complicated and exhausting, and the ceremony for the exorcism of my ghost, conducted by my uncle Joe in his hogan on the reservation, was no exception. My mother and father and Kiko were all present, as well as my mother's good friend my honorary "aunt" Cindy and my half brother Charles (this was the period when he was living with my mother and father in their trailer at the A-1 storage facility in Santa Fe). In addition to being long and complicated, Navajo ceremonies are also extremely sacred and private, and I really should not reveal much about this one except to say that it was at times terrifying and at times painful—and that it seemed to do the trick. When it was all over, Uncle Joe informed us that the woman had been a potentially harmful ghost. He said that when my mother was pregnant with me, she and my father had driven past an accident on the highway just as a woman who had been injured in the accident was dying. He said the woman's spirit had crawled into my mother's womb with me. As I think about all of this now, it occurs to me for the first time that perhaps this was why my mother felt me "dancing" in her womb before I was born.

By April 2003 I had rid myself of the Tiresome Catholic, and just a month later I seemed to have also rid myself of the annoying spirit who had been stalking me for years. As a result, on June 15, 2003, when I walked into a New York restaurant and watering hole called the Park one sultry summer night to have a nightcap with my friend Jason, I was finally a free man. Thank God, because that was the night I looked across the room and saw Luis. He was standing near the bar, wearing a suit and tie, looking very dashing holding his ice-cold lager. Everyone else was wearing shorts and T-shirts. I was feeling flirty, so I approached him and said, "So what's with the suit?"

Luis has an accent that sounds formal and old-fashioned, as if he were born perhaps from Spanish royalty. (When I tease him about this now he always gives me that glare, as if to say, "It's not funny, because I *am* royalty!") He told me, in his elegant, rich voice, that he had just gotten off from work. When I continued with my questions I discovered that he was a chef and a sommelier, and that he had studied at the Culinary Institute of America.

I was immediately taken (and I still am) by Luis's beauty—his dark hair, his dark eyes, the dimples, that voice—and by the blend of confidence and kindness and panache he exuded: he seemed to be a dashing blend of James Bond, Robin Hood, and a Spanish musketeer rolled into one gorgeous, modern gay man. We were both performing standard bar flirtation that night, but I also sensed instantly, at that very first meeting, that something profound was happening and that Luis and I would be a part of each other's futures.

Luis and I had our first date that same week, at the restaurant Gramercy Tavern. I was dancing that evening—as always—so of course it had to be a late dinner. I told Luis that I would arrange a ticket for him for that evening's performance of the ballet, but he insisted on buying his own ticket. That impressed me. When we sat down at our table in Gramercy Tavern and our waiter approached, I ordered a glass of chardonnay. I thought I saw Luis flinch—had I done something wrong? I am a real ditz about remembering people's names, or anything else they tell me upon first meeting, and I had forgotten everything from Luis's and my first encounter, including the fact that he was a professional chef and sommelier. (To be honest, I think I was too busy looking to listen.) There was a slight silence, after which Luis ordered a gin and tonic. When the waiter returned with our drinks, he also brought with him a bottle of La Tâche burgundy—Luis had had it sent over from the restaurant where he worked. I didn't recognize the wine by its name, but my first sip told me all I needed to know. I had already been impressed that Luis had insisted on buying his own ticket to the ballet; that extraordinary bottle of La Tâche impressed me once more.

As Luis and I got to know each other over the next few weeks we quickly discovered our mutual love of cooking, and then had fun performing our respective and very different culinary styles for each other. I was the first to display my skills. As a cook, I am a self-taught amateur, with a talent for improvisation and shortcuts (I could probably do a whole cookbook of recipes that have Campbell's soup as the secret ingredient). For my opening act, I cooked Luis a roast chicken, with mashed potatoes and frozen peas. He insisted that he loved it.

Luis, as I've mentioned, is a professional chef, thoroughly trained in the best tradition. The first meal he prepared for me was a sautéed fillet of sockeye salmon in a crunchy, armored crust of thinly sliced potatoes, served on a bed of leeks with a beurre blanc sauce and a triumphant final topping of caviar. I was knocked out. And of course I will never forget our first Christmas together. Luis insisted on doing everything for the Christmas dinner. First he shopped for all the ingredients in the city, and then spent three days making a demi-glace— which left our city bathtub full of stock bones. On Christmas Eve we transported the holy demi-glace and the holiday groceries to the Connecticut house, and on Christmas Day Luis set about the business of making our holiday dinner while I busied myself with other duties. When I finally peeked into the kitchen I almost had a heart attack. It was a complete war zone. Every bowl, every pot, every pan, and every spoon had been used.

Luis looked up at me and smiled. "I'm done!" he exclaimed, clapping his hands three times. "Oh no, you're not," I thought to myself, as I surveyed the incredible chaos and destruction. But the Christmas meal that year was absolutely sublime, and I quickly realized that supreme talent sometimes comes with a cost. In addition to our passion for food, Luis and I soon discovered a shared passion for the performing arts: he was all about opera and I was all about ballet, but once again our different areas of expertise complemented each other.

After Luis and I got to know each other better we moved in together, and a series of positive changes and a sorely needed sense of stability came into my life. We lived at first in a tiny but charming walk-up studio in an old building on Eleventh Street in the Village, above a restaurant called Gene's. Gene's is about a hundred years old—seriously, and I think some of the patrons have been eating there since the place opened. It serves a mean vodka martini in a glass that always reminds me of a goldfish bowl. The owners are very pleasant and they used to lend Luis and me little round tables for the small dinner parties we often hosted.

Stability couldn't have come at a better time for me. Luis's presence and our domestic life together was a huge comfort and support to me later that year when my mother was diagnosed with cancer and had to undergo a series of operations. And it was Luis who helped me through the difficult walk-up to my retirement. I had reached an odd point in my career, because in many ways I was doing some of the most interesting work I had ever done. In addition to Chris's new ballets, I was partnering Darci in several new ballets by Peter—such as the very sexy and provocative *Guide to Strange Places* and his *Tālā Gaisma*. Between my commitments for the regular season, I was still being booked on fascinating trips abroad and special gigs at home. My understanding of my art was more intricate and sophisticated than ever—but, undeniably, my body was breaking down. I tore each of my calf muscles several times in my last years at NYCB, and coming back got rougher each time. Often I would have to skip rehearsals, or instead walk through my pas de deux briefly and then spend the rest of the day getting my body ready for that night's performance. The performances were still sublimely exciting. But the pain afterward was extreme. It's terrible to have to let go of the thing you love most in the world—but I knew the time for change was coming.

. . . .

MY LIFE TOOK an important new direction on that June evening in 2003 when I met Luis at the Park. At the time I never would have guessed that five years later, in the King Cole Bar at New York's St. Regis Hotel, my whole life would change dramatically once again. On that evening Luis and I and our friend Nancy had just finished a delicious dinner at Il Convivio, and Luis talked us into stopping at the St. Regis for a nightcap. After arriving and settling in, I made a quick trip to the men's room, and when I returned, Luis—in pure Luis form—had ordered a bottle of '95 Krug champagne. He had also pushed aside the table from in front of our sofa and was down on one knee. I looked at Nancy quizzically as I sat down, and then at Luis. He gave me a big smile, and then he produced a beautiful ring and proposed.

I was absolutely stunned—so stunned that the first thing to come out of my mouth was, "You've gotta be fucking kidding me!" Perhaps not the reaction Luis was hoping for. So then he asked me if that response was a yes or a no. (He later confessed that he had asked Nancy to be there with us that evening because he was so nervous about proposing.) I immediately shouted, "Yes!" And then I began to sob. It wasn't until the waiter came over and said, "Congratulations" that I realized that this was all actually happening. And then I began to sob even harder.

In all the years that I have lived in New York I never thought that I would get married. Even in this modern and sophisticated city, the notion of two men getting married still seems to be strange to many people. (Though I have to admit, in recent years when I have browsed through the marriage announcements in the Sunday *Times* and spotted a picture of two recently married men, I've sometimes shed a secret tear.) I cannot believe that in my midforties, more than three decades after my father caught me dancing in front of the mirror and lip-synching to "People" from *Funny Girl*, I am finally going to be Sadie, the married lady. I have never been so happy.

The day after Luis and I got engaged I decided to say nothing about my news at school, but I noticed the boys eyeing my ring finger all day. In my last class, when I saw two of them sort of nudging each other, I asked what was going on. One of them approached me shyly and asked about my bling. I couldn't hold back. I confessed that, yes, in fact, I was engaged—and when they all broke into wild applause, of course my eyes filled with tears again. It is an unusual family I have built for myself here in New York, but a close one and a dear one. I explained to the boys how Luis had contacted my friend Johnny Reinhold, the art collector and jeweler whom I'd known since my Warhol days, and had him design a ring with thirty-seven black diamonds set in white gold, and with one ruby on the inside (for Luis). It is an exquisite ring, to celebrate the beautiful life we hope to have together. I know how much my mother loved Luis, and I only wish that she could be alive to share in this happy moment, too.

Everything in life can feel so haphazard and arbitrary at times, but as I get older and as I examine things more carefully I am beginning to realize how beautiful and complex our relationships become over the years. I can see this both in my family of origin with its sprawling clan of aunts and

uncles and cousins that still lives primarily in the western territories where I was born, and in my eclectic adoptive family
of NYCB colleagues and other friends here in New York.
Over the years my two branches of family have intersected
and intertwined in many ways, and members of each branch
have been with me through many of the challenges and triumphs, as well as the trials and disappointments, that life has
dealt. Now that we have a house in New Mexico that we visit
when we can, the various relationships in my once very separate worlds of dance and family seem to be cross-pollinating
more and more. I find it fascinating the way love and trust
and acceptance and forgiveness grow with and through the
important relationships we forge in life, and how even occur-
rences that may at first feel like happenstance often become
part of a profound and beautiful design. As I write this I am
reminded of Pop's story of how he and Mom first met in a
bar that played salsa music, and how he knew right away that
they were meant to be together. Life can be so haphazard—
and it also seems that, in my family at least, it can be a risky
move to visit bars. If you step out for a quick drink with a
friend you may wind up changing your entire future. In my
case, not a day passes that I don't thank God for my One Last
Nightcap at the Park.

A New Year's Eve Feast and Dance Party

WHEN LUIS AND I were first living together in our tiny studio apartment, we used to throw small dinner parties for friends all the time. But the year I retired from NYCB we decided to try something more ambitious—a New Year's Eve party for twenty-two. We moved all of our furniture into the hallway, rented two twelve-foot tables, blocked off the kitchen with a curtain we nailed up, and sat everyone formally.

I remember it being one hell of a night. We served scallops with two sauces, filet mignon with Luis's gorgeous demiglace and morels, sautéed green beans, and Gruyère scalloped potatoes with tons of cream and garlic. For dessert we had crème brûlée. After dinner we all danced until the sun came up, and then we collapsed. It took us about a week to clean up the mess, but it was judged by all to have been a fine way to launch the New Year. So fine, in fact, that Luis and I have hosted a similar party every year since. The main entrée changes from year to year—sometimes we do a roast lamb or a beef Wellington or a turkey instead of filet mignon—but one dish that remains a constant is the Gruyère scalloped potatoes. Rich, creamy, and oozing with cheese, this dish makes any meal seem significant. People can never get enough.

Gruyère Scalloped Potatoes

SERVES 8 GENEROUSLY

This is a recipe that I have been making for years, but recently Luis showed me a great shortcut. You place the sliced potatoes in the cream before it's scalded and start the cooking process on top of the stove, and then transfer them to an ovenproof casserole, add cheese, and bake.

2 cups heavy cream

4 pounds russet potatoes

6 cloves garlic, finely
    minced (a lot more if you
    love garlic)

2 teaspoons salt

1 teaspoon ground white
    pepper

A pinch (just a pinch!)
    freshly grated nutmeg

½ stick butter, softened

2 cups grated Gruyère

Preheat the oven to 400 degrees.

In a large pot, carefully bring the cream to a slight simmer, and then turn off the heat.

Peel the potatoes and cut them into about ⅛-inch slices (you can slice them thinner if you happen to have a mandoline, but never, ever use the slicer attachment of your food processor). Drop the sliced potatoes into the scalded cream as you work, to prevent them from turning color. Add the garlic, salt, pepper, and nutmeg with the potatoes and cream, and mix well with your hands.

Spread the butter all over a large ovenproof casserole to grease it, and pour in the potatoes and cream mixture. Top the assembly with the Gruyère, cover the casserole with foil, and bake for about 1 hour. Remove the foil, and continue baking for another 45 minutes—if the top starts to go past the "golden brown" point, cover with the foil again.

You'll know the gratin is done if you pierce it in the middle with a knife and the knife pulls away with no resistance. It's preferable to let it cool for about half an hour so it won't be too runny—but I have never known anybody to object if this is not possible.

NOTE: For fancier presentations or do-ahead dinner parties, let the gratin cool to room temperature, and refrigerate it overnight. The next day, you can cut the gratin into squares or ovals using a cookie cutter and wrap them individually in foil. To reheat, place them on a greased sheet pan in a preheated 425-degree oven for about 30 minutes. They will hold their shape beautifully and you can plate them easily.

CHAPTER FIFTEEN

Coda

When you get, give. . . . When you learn, teach.
—ANNIE HENDERSON, MAYA ANGELOU'S GRANDMOTHER

When I think back on my retirement performance on June 19, 2005, I often find myself in the moment when Wendy and I were getting ready to go onstage for our last performance together, dancing the pas de deux from *After the Rain*, the ballet Chris had choreographed on us only six months earlier. Operating on pure adrenaline—flying through costume changes and getting quick massages for cramps in my hands and legs between ballets—I had already danced Jerome Robbins's *West Side Story Suite*, Peter Martins's *Barber Violin Concerto*, and Lynne Taylor-Corbett's *Chiaroscuro*. I had two ballets to go. I wasn't sure what would happen.

Wendy had acknowledged by then, in both media interviews and in our own conversations, that she felt "shook up" about the end of our partnership. I felt "shook up," too, and especially so at that moment. For a dancer, the process of performing can be so unpredictable and tumultuous, and so many of the emotions that go coursing through the Bermuda Triangle of body and mind and spirit are unavailable to the tidy world of spoken words. But Wendy and I had found a language for sharing our emotions, and a way to float in and out and around the physical and spiritual beings we each encompassed, allowing our two beings to merge into one. I doubted I would ever again find an experience like the one I was about to share with Wendy, one last time, and the finality of that fact and that moment seemed almost incomprehensible.

Wendy and I stepped onstage, and as we stood there waiting for the curtain to go up, I hugged her. She hugged me back. I said to her what I had always said to her before we began, "It's going to be a different story tonight." And she said back, as she had always done, "I will meet you there." The curtain lifted and the moment we began to dance I knew that I had nothing to worry about. Wendy and I stepped into the world where music and movement meet, as we always have, and we danced a new story—a story that existed only once, right there on that stage, in that moment of time.

As I finished my last, tender, heart-wrenching pas de deux with the sublime Wendy Whelan I got a glimpse of the whole company standing in the wings, waiting to join me for the fifth and final piece, the "Royal Navy" section of George Balanchine's *Union Jack*. I tried not to think about the fact that this was the last time I would share the stage with all of my amazing colleagues, who had become dear friends and my surrogate family here in New York, but it was such an emotional moment for me as I changed into my little sailor suit backstage and then headed out. My fellow dancers and I

threw ourselves around the stage with wild and giddy abandon, on the verge of giggles and tears all at once it seemed.
We did our big leaps and turns, and we waltzed and horn-
piped and jigged our way through the killing emotion of it
all—and then, with a robust finale from the orchestra pit, it
was over. The audience was roaring, an avalanche of flowers was descending upon the stage, everyone was in tears. As
I stood there, numb with sadness and so many other emotions, I looked out once more to find my family in the nearby
orchestra seats, and once again caught my mother's eye and
basked in her smile.

A few minutes later, when I finally got to give my mother
and father a hug backstage, my mother lingered in my arms,
leaning against my chest. "I'm exhausted," she said, tears running down her cheeks. "I was sending you all my strength."
I could feel her exhaustion, and I knew that what she said
was true. She guided me through this day as she had guided
me, even from a distance, through almost every step of my
life. I straightened her wig and the two of us giggled while
crying into each other's necks, weeping as if I had just fought
a world war. And then, though I have never been one to brag,
I granted myself my own highest praise. I smiled at my parents and said, "It went well."

The infinite potential for creativity that dance offers is
what has fascinated and nourished me for years, and it was
the unparalleled thrill of expressing such creativity moment
by moment onstage that I most dreaded losing on that June
night when I retired as a performing dancer. Would I have
the appetite and the openness and the enterprise to find another pursuit that would let me tell a different story every

day? Would I have the good luck to find people like Wendy and Heather and Darci and all the other gifted dancers I had worked with over the years, whom I could love and trust and with whom I could share the wonder of it all? And if the answers to the first two questions were no, would I be able to stand it? In the months leading up to and immediately after my retirement, all of these questions seemed so upsetting I didn't let myself think about them much. I kept my head down and marched forward.

But one of the things I have discovered since retiring is that some of our most important lessons in life can only be fully absorbed in hindsight. I can see now that during all those months when I thought I was avoiding the tough questions about my future, I was also gathering answers to those same questions. I remember a period when Luis and I were first together, for instance, when we would sometimes argue the comparative merits of ballet versus opera. Luis is a huge opera fan, and I, of course, at that point at least, was ballet all the way. I did not understand Luis's obsession with opera—I was used to seeing gorgeous bodies dancing around, creating impossible visions. And I particularly didn't understand his obsession with Wagner. As a result, when he decided early in our relationship to take me to my first Wagner opera—*Tristan und Isolde*, an opera that runs a marathon five hours—I was very dubious. I didn't have a clear idea of what I was about to experience, but I was quite certain I wasn't going to like it.

Five hours later, when the curtain fell after the final aria, I was completely overwhelmed with emotion. I was shaking and tears were running down my face. The beauty of the singing and the glorious sound of the orchestra had taken me completely by surprise and had moved me deeply, both emotionally and physically. I was amazed at the magic I had just witnessed, and stunned by the talent and stamina the artists had displayed. Within the passage of those five hours I had come to understand the beauty of opera, and appreciate the hard work and purity of expression it must take to reach a level of artistry such as I had just seen.

The feelings that overcame me at that performance of *Tristan und Isolde*, I realize as I recall the experience now, are almost identical to the feelings that overcame me when I watched Peter Martins lead Suzanne Farrell onto the stage to perform the second movement of *Symphony in C* on the day of Balanchine's death. And this simple discovery—that is, that different experiences in life can be linked by the quality and the kind of emotions they evoke—is both amazing and liberating. It suggests, among other things, that there are many different paths to many different fine places in life.

Finding and exploring these many paths is what I have been trying to do since retiring as a dancer, and I am happy to report that if you are alert and open and interested, you can find many opportunities for creativity and meaningful expression every day in this long dance called life. On June 20, 2005, the morning after the day I retired, I began my classes at the Institute of Culinary Education and a year later I had my degree in restaurant business management—just as I had planned. I have always enjoyed cooking, but now more than ever I understand the ways in which the disciplined and applied art of cooking resembles that of choreography and dancing. All three are about the quality of the ingredients used, the creativity that goes into the way they are combined, and the timing and precision with which the prescribed actions are executed. All of them involve performances that have a beginning, a middle, and an end—as does the career of a dancer. Of course, the parallels between cooking and dance are not unknown. Balanchine's love of food and his dedication to the art of cooking were renowned. When Mr. B's fourth wife, Tanaquil Le Clercq, published *The Ballet Cook Book*, she quoted Balanchine on the qualifications of a true cook: "No matter what he does, he must not rush, yet he must not be late, and the finished product must be exquisite. You need patience, and finally you have to appease your public's appetite. Besides this, it should be inexpensive enough to be accessible, and, in itself, the whole must be pretty and there must be a lot of it." The same qualifications, of course, might easily be applied to the challenge of creating a successful ballet company!

For Luis and me, working together in the kitchen has become a kind of secondary partnership—a performing partnership. We love entertaining our friends—it knits our worlds together—and we do some catering when our schedules allow it. In September 2005, shortly after I retired, we catered Wendy Whelan's wedding to David Michalek. It was a complete joy. That same year we threw a New Year's Eve party for twenty-two in our tiny walk-up studio. I remember it being quite a party, with five courses and an array of fine wines. We asked each of our guests to bring a bottle of Veuve Clicquot—we all laughed when little Yvonne Borree brought a magnum, almost too big for her to carry, and tall, handsome Amar Ramasar brought a split—and we put all twenty-two bottles in an ice chest. At about 2 a.m. we folded the tables and put them aside so that we could all dance. I can still picture Wendy jumping up and down on my couch wearing a big New Year's top hat.

Teaching my ballet classes at SAB is another major path that allows me to participate in the kind of creative alchemy that I experienced when dancing. My classes with my students always excite me—I am continually amazed and thrilled by their talents and accomplishments, and I am always learning as much as they are. Ironically, I often find myself using cooking metaphors to critique their exercises. "Don't stir her like a pot of soup! She is not a pot of soup!" I screamed at one poor boy the other day. "Don't stand there like a frozen fish stick," I told another. When an ensemble exercise with eighteen boys was horridly executed I stopped them and scolded: "You're not supposed to look like popcorn!" "This is a drumroll, this is a magic act," I often remind them. "It has to look like something, and every step you take has to mean something."

I am struck more and more these days by how privileged I was, and am, to be a part of this school that was Lincoln Kirstein's beautiful idea and George Balanchine's dearest dream. It all begins in the classroom, and all of us who teach at SAB believe it is our duty to carry on and expand the legacy of Balanchine's vision and art. Peter Martins and Kay Mazzo believe this. Darci Kistler, who was Balanchine's "last ballerina," and who retired as a dancer in 2009, believes it. Andrei Kramarevsky, who once taught me, and who is in his eighties and still teaching, believes it. I believe it. Witnessing the beauty of this continuation, as students learn to perform with dignity and pride, is always an emotional and deeply moving experience, and I find watching them perform in choreography workshops, where students work with students to create new pieces, particularly inspiring. It is wonderful to see the innocence and joy they bring to every moment of their performance, and to know that nobody can ever take that feeling away from them.

I sometimes try to explain to my students that they are all at SAB for a reason, and that this is the starting point of an incredible journey that can transform them into true artists. It all begins in the classroom. Dancing can't have an ego, I tell them, and it will not make them millionaires. But they will have an opportunity to share and touch a part of Balanchine's legacy—or, as Darci sometimes says, the "fairy dust." As a teacher I sometimes get to watch a talented student or young company member metamorphose, in the course of a single performance, into a real artist. It can happen onstage in an instant. It's amazing—boom! Suddenly she is a full-blown ballerina, or he is a brilliant principal. What a thrilling and magical process to witness. Miraculous, even. It is moments like this that make me realize how blessed I have been.

As I look back now over the years since I retired, I am actually pleasantly surprised by how many different paths to different stories I have already explored. In addition to my cooking and my full-time teaching at SAB and making the documentary *Water Flowing Together* with Gwendolen Cates, I have been invited to give talks on various dance topics, conduct workshops on partnering, and travel to different places as a visiting artist. In 2006 I went to London for three weeks to stage *Afternoon of a Faun* for the Robbins Foundation with the Royal Ballet; in 2007, to my great delight, I got to work once more with Peter Martins—probably the most important and influential man in my life besides Luis, and one who still calls me his "second son"—choreographing a new ballet. I played Lord Capulet to Darci's Lady Capulet in NYCB'S new *Romeo and Juliet*. I have begun to choreograph a few pieces, both for the school and for other forums, and every year I get the special treat of traveling around the country to audition kids for the school. It is always so thrilling to spot new talent, and it always takes me back to those days long ago when I myself was a little boy with big dreams.

One of my most interesting projects since retiring—and an experience that brought me back full circle to my own heritage—came when I was a guest teacher at the Banff Centre for the Arts, teaching classical ballet to Native American dancers. Most of my students had never had any experience with classical ballet, and I was impressed by how eager they were to learn—they did not have a single shy bone among them. I was also impressed by the amazing natural rhythm they had, in their bodies and in their souls. It was palpable. It has always been a dream of mine to find a way to help young Native Americans understand that it is okay to leave the reservation—that it is possible to have big dreams and to pursue them and to change your life.

Since my mother's death, the process of reexamining my life and reaching beyond the world of Lincoln Center has taken me on so many journeys, and opened me up to new experiences and new ways of thinking that I would never have expected to encounter. I have been asked, for instance, to host assorted arts events for a local television network, and recently two film producers followed Luis and me through the steps of one of our catering jobs (we honored our puppy, Tristan, by naming our company "Lucky Basset") to film a pilot for a potential cooking show. Another example of the new frontiers I am exploring involves what has previously been an awkward topic for me—spirituality and faith. For a time when I was little my parents used to drop Kiko and me at Sunday school every week in Arizona, but they never stayed to attend the church services themselves. (I have always assumed this was their way of getting some private time to have sex.) In my years as a free-roaming ballet wolf cub in New York I certainly never attended church, and Balanchine was the only god I ever acknowledged. For years I made the sign of the cross every time I was about to go onstage to perform, but that was more about superstition and repetitive motion than religion. But now, in my midforties, I feel I am gaining some perspective on a deeper and more spiritual way of life. I find I have a greater desire to share my thoughts and feelings with others, to communicate with and understand others— in my job as a teacher and in my outside life as well. " 'Bout time," Mom would probably say.

We have finally finished building the house in New Mexico—"Mama Jo's house," as we all call it—thereby gaining initiation into the mixed bag of thrills and horrors that comes with home building and home ownership. The more time I spend at this house the more I am struck by the exceptional skies and landscapes that surround it—the dramatic mixes of storm clouds and rainbows, the gushes of wind that set the brilliant yellow aspen trees dancing, the shimmering shiny blue and dark blue tapestry of the lake surface, which changes texture constantly throughout the day. I know it is odd for someone like me, who has spent his whole life running away from the reservation and my Navajo heritage, to be looking out at the same land now with such curiosity and passion. But everything looks so alive—I feel I could watch it forever. When I am out there I love taking long hikes and steeping myself in the natural beauty of the surrounding mountains; every expedition tells me a different story, even if I am walking the same trail. I have begun to make friends with my neighbors in this tiny town, and they are all kind and fun and full of fascinating information about experiences from all over the world. For the first time I am opening up to the comforts and joys of an alternate home base in a place far away from New York City.

In the first months after Mom died I felt like the world had gone on intermission, and I was passively waiting for the performance to start up and come to its conclusion. I feel that way much less often now, and there are many days when I feel that I am back onstage and a part of a vibrant performance. Possibly my mother herself is guiding me to this spiritual place, but step-by-step I am learning how to live without her for the time being—I know I will be with her again someday. And day by day my father has begun to play a more important role in my life. I make frequent trips to the house, where we spend time together, and whenever I go to Albuquerque to audition students for the SAB summer course, I see Pop. He picks me up at the airport and drives me to the Eagle Nest house. I cook for him and organize his things and make his room comfortable. All those years that he drove me to ballet class and bought me ballet shoes and tights—he deserves some rest and relaxation.

Losing my mother has undoubtedly been the greatest trial I have had to bear so far in my life, but it has brought important lessons. The first of these—that we are all mortal, and that our time here is our most precious possession—is the most obvious. My mother's long illness, stressful and sad as it was, had the upside of drawing many of the far-flung members of my extended family together; our shared love for her will continue after her death. Kiko's sons, Trevor and Bryce, are in constant communication with all of us now, and for the first time ever my father and I are growing close.

Recently we buried Mom's ashes at the foot of a beautiful pine tree that stands in front of the Eagle Nest house—a tree in honor of my mother, in a land my mother honored. I imagine this tree growing to be the tallest tree in the valley. I remember reading that Native Americans believe trees are vibrant with energy and call them our "standing brothers." This tree will be my standing mother, overlooking the valley and protecting us the way she always has. Next year, when I host a family reunion at Mama Jo's house in Eagle Nest, I will make sure that all of her siblings attend. This will be my family hoop dance—getting all of us in one place together, with my mother watching over us from her little nest beneath the pine tree.

It has been more than three years now since Mom died, and more than five years since I left the stage. On the morning that marked the second anniversary of Mom's death—March

25, 2010—I was making coffee in the kitchen when I heard the music from Balanchine's *Brahms-Schoenberg Quartet* (the Brahms Piano Quartet in G minor, as orchestrated by Arnold Schoenberg) on the radio. I may have been a little sentimental because of thoughts of my mother, but the sound of the music brought me to tears—and it brought back such beautiful memories. I danced three of the movements of that piece when I was in the company. I was lucky enough to be cast by Peter to do the third movement with Darci when I was very young. Later on, I danced the second movement with Patricia McBride, and then with Heather. And, finally, I danced the fourth movement with Monique Meunier and Kyra Nichols. Each of these roles was different in its way, and each was danced differently with each partner each time we performed. The astounding beauty and freedom and opportunity embraced by this one ballet—it all seems to me as wide as the universe. All of this beauty and freedom is what I had wanted for as long as I can remember. And thanks to my parents and a cast of brilliant teachers, choreographers, dancers, and students, all of this I received.

As I look back on a story that meanders from a remote region in the Arizona desert through three turbulent decades in Manhattan and the world at large, I am overwhelmed by the passion and gratitude I feel for the experiences I have had, both as a dancer with the New York City Ballet and as a member of my family. I can see that both experiences have been a crucial part of who I am today, and I am more and more comfortable with the decisions I have made in my life. I did leave the reservation; I did separate from my family at a young age to pursue a personal dream—but this is okay.

I have had a wonderful life thus far, and there is still much more to come. Again, I wish there was a way I could tell every little boy and girl—not just those out on the reservation where I grew up, but everywhere—that it is okay to dream, and to dream big. The paths you can follow through life are as infinite as the stars that populate the desert night sky. And while I may be the product of a confusing mix of influences, with every day that passes I feel more confident and proud of that mix: I can now say with complete confidence that I am one very happy, very lucky Navarican-Puertojo-desert-born-New-York-bred-gay-recently-engaged-part-time-cook-fledgling-choreographer-proud-first-time-home-owner-recently-published-author-retired-dancer-ballet-teacher. Oh—did I mention that I have a first name of Hebrew origin and the last name of a man who is not my grandfather? To celebrate all my happiness and my good fortune and my bright hopes for the future, I am thinking of printing up a new business card that reads:

Jock Soto
Searching for Stories, Will Travel

Acknowledgments

There is no way that I would have ever considered writing this book at the time that it was suggested. I received a letter proposing a book shortly after my mother had passed away. It had been only a few months since her death, and the only thing on my mind was how I could possibly live without her.

Out of curiosity, I agreed to a meeting at Gelfman Schneider. It was a hot day, and I regrettably decided to ride my bicycle to their Midtown offices from Lincoln Center, where I was between teaching classes. I arrived soaked, wearing bicycle shorts, a tank top, and, consequently, a bad mood.

Someone there had seen the documentary about me and decided there might be more to tell. I wasn't sure I agreed. After some prodding, I politely said I would think about it. And besides, if I felt like writing anything, it would only be as a tribute to my mother.

On my way back to the school, I found myself remembering so much of my past, perhaps exhilarated by the prospect of this project or maybe delirious from the scorching sun. I had a few hours to spare before my next class and was surprised when I had already written thirty pages in the faculty's dressing room. There was more to tell, after all.

A thank-you to my beautiful love and partner and to our hounds, Tristan and Bandit. When you think that love is lost, a miracle can come. I look at him as my true love and my partner in a pas de deux about understanding how you get to share something with someone who is also your best friend. Luis, my love for life, my love for love, thank you for understanding and having the patience to come into my life and loving me through all the hardships and being there to hold me up whenever I need your strength.

When we feel that everything has gone bad, we look at our dogs and think what they could be thinking. It's usually, "Where is my food?" I'm sure. So we cook them a morsel of something that is as great as what we are eating. Why can't a special beast eat what we have the pleasure of having? Dogs only cock their heads and wait for you to give them love or praise. Think about what they do for us: we can't wait to come home to them, and they can't wait to eat and poop. Still, they are the most loyal. My loyalty is to my little family and friends in New York, and I cherish it. It is what I have, and it is what I do.

To my mother and father, Mama Jo and Papa Joe, for the faith and belief in taking a child to ballet class and not thinking it was a waste of time. My beautiful and powerful mother will always be my strength, and my love for her will never die. To my father for driving me for countless hours even when we weren't speaking and for supporting me when I thought I couldn't dance anymore. And now, for taking care of the house that Luis and I built and watching over my mother's fenced-in chosen burial site in New Mexico. To my brother, Kiko, for being the rock when I was growing up—and being my rock to this day—when I needed a bodyguard as I was walked to school, and not being embarrassed when I danced around in parking lots, and letting me put his legs in ballet positions while our family laughed. To Kiko's wife, Deb, for being my mother's strength and helping her through some of the hardest times at the end of her life and for being the sister I never had.

To the Fuentes family for being my extended relatives, and to Mrs. Fuentes for saying that she is my mother, too, and will be always. To my early and inspiring teachers: Kelly Brown, Isabel Brown, Irina Kosmovska, Yvonne Mounsey, and Rosemary Valaire. To my teacher Brian Buckley at the Institute of Culinary Education here in New York after I retired. Going back to school at age forty was a hoot, and I made some great friends out of it. To my teachers at the School of American Ballet, the wonderful and amazing teacher Stanley Williams, Richard Rapp, and Andrei Kramarevsky, who still teaches to this day.

Of course, colossal and undying gratitude to George Balanchine, who invited me to join his company and paved my future. I will always be in awe of his ballets. Every time I see his ballets, something new happens, and that's what keeps anyone who loves ballet inspired. That is enough to keep any teacher going—to pass on what you learn is best. Thanks to Jerome Robbins. He was a perfectionist, and if you didn't deliver it was difficult. That's where patience became even more of a challenge, but when you got it right, it was worth it. Both are geniuses along with Peter Martins, my guide and surrogate father, my friend, my director, and my boss. I was raised in the New York City Ballet, and the trust he and I have for each other will never fade. He gave me so much, and in return I am faithful and grateful. Peter introduced me to so many new ways of partnering and dancing, and we continue to teach, share, and learn. What could be better? So many ballets, so many memories. I teach at the school because of Peter, and I thank him every day for that. My love for him will never die: thank you! His beautiful wife, the last Balanchine ballerina, my colleague Darci Kistler, with whom I teach now and had the pleasure of sharing so many wonderful works. Lots of great moments onstage together, lots of great meals to come. To Wendy Whelan for being Wendy—I loves ya! What an inspiring being and what a treasure to a great company. To Heather Watts for everything you can possibly imagine. To all of the beautiful ballerinas with whom I had the pleasure of dancing! To Kay Mazzo and the School of American Ballet, with which I have made a full circle and where I enjoy teaching every day.

I never would have even considered writing this book if my literary agent, Heather Mitchell, at Gelfman Schneider hadn't talked me into it that hot day. I trust her and respect her opinion. She's also sexy as hell! To Erin Arbuckle, for her generous help with research. To Bob Miller, who at the time planted the seed for the book. To Rakesh Satyal, who is my editor and believed in this book from the first day he read it, and I especially love that he moonlights as a performer!

Finally, I have to thank Leslie Marshall, whose writing and organizational skills surpass everything. She is my best friend, and Luis and I are proud to be godparents to her beautiful children; there are not enough thank-yous for what she had to do as I threw pages her way that I couldn't even read. The endless texts and e-mails that, if I look back on them, make me sound like a lunatic. She knows me better than I know myself. When I said yes to this book, I couldn't think of anyone else who could help me do this. The blood, sweat, and tears she had to endure, listen to, and read must have been enough for a call to a psychiatrist. When making dinner side by side in Bellport we would talk about stories of my past and she would remember every word I said. Meanwhile, I can't remember what I ate yesterday for lunch.

She became me, and at one point when we were all getting ready for bed in Bellport I remember I ran to her bedroom and saw that we were wearing the same turquoise Calvin Klein underwear. I know—weird but true. Leslie, my godsend. My mother would have loved sitting and talking with you. My dreams see the two of you doing what you and I do now. Standing at a counter preparing meals for our families, having a gorgeous glass of wine from one of the bottles Luis has brought. Listening to the crackling of the perfect fire in the fireplace that your husband, Billy, has made. Watching all of our dogs lying around the fire waiting for a treat. The godchildren, Jo, Bea, and Marshall, laughing and playing some board game. Then we go to the beach and have a bonfire while everyone sings along to songs from our past while staring at the stars and the ocean. What could be better than that? Thank you, Leslie. I love you.